Also by Leslie Fiedler

Fiedler on the Roof

Fiedler on the Roof

ESSAYS ON LITERATURE

AND JEWISH IDENTITY

Leslie Fiedler

 DAVID R. GODINE, PUBLISHER
BOSTON

First published in 1991 by
DAVID R. GODINE, PUBLISHER, INC.
Horticultural Hall
300 Massachusetts Avenue
Boston, Massachusetts 02115

First printed in softcover in 1992

Library of Congress Cataloging-in-Publication Data
Fielder, Leslie A.
    Fiedler on the roof : essays / by Leslie Fielder—1st ed.
        p.   cm.
    Contents: The roots of anti-Semitism : a view from Italy—Bloom
on Joyce, or, Jokey for Jacob—Joyce and Jewish consciousness—
The Christian-ness of the Jewish-American writer—Isaac Bashevis
Singer, or, The American-ness of the American-Jewish writer—Why
is the grail knight Jewish? : a Passover meditation—William
Styron's Sophie's choice—Going for the long ball—Growing up
post-Jewish—the many names of S. Levin : an essay in genre
criticism—a meditation of the Book of Job—In every generation
: a meditation on the two Holocausts.
    ISBN 0-87923-859-3 (HC)
    ISBN 0-87923-949-2 (SC)
    I. Title.
PS3556.I34F5   1990   90-55282
814'.54—dc20   CIP

First softcover printing, 1992
Printed in the United State of America

"In blood, in blood shalt thou remember . . ."

Contents

Preface

For nearly twenty years now I have been writing less and less about Jewish-American novelists like Saul Bellow, Bernard Malamud, and Philip Roth. Indeed, I no longer read their newest fiction with the sense of discovery and delight that led me to tout so extravagantly their earlier work, eventually helping to make it a part of the canon and to win for it an ever-growing audience both Jewish and goyish, not just in America but throughout the world. It was not, I realize now, a disinterested venture, since I thought of myself at the beginning of my writing career as part of the movement that had carried such children of immigrant Jews from Eastern Europe from the periphery to the center of American literary culture—making their experience, *our* experience, a part of the communal dream stuff, the myth that makes all Americans one, whatever their ethnic origin.

Such a development seemed to me (as I patiently explained

in print and from the lecture platform) inevitable at the moment just after World War II, not only because the revelations about the horrors of the Nazi concentration camps and the news about the improbable battlefield victories of the new State of Israel had created a wave of philo-Semitism in the United States. It was also a time of growing alienation and rapid urbanization, which made the Jews, experts on exile and the indignities of city life, appropriate spokesmen for everyone. I have scarcely been surprised, therefore, that in the decades since, along with Jewish archetypal images, the cadences of an English influenced, however remotely, by Yiddish have passed into the public domain. So, too, certain Yiddish words (once needing footnotes in the texts where they originally appeared) have entered our common vocabulary, so that scarcely anyone does not know what *chutzpah* is, or cannot tell the difference between a *maven* and a *schlemiel.*

At the same moment, moreover, that our language and our dreams were being thus altered by Jewish-American artists (on stage and screen, as well as in print), our very notions of our literary past have been radically changed by Jewish-American critics—some of them without academic credentials, like Philip Rahv, Alfred Kazin, and Irving Howe; some quite proper academics, like Harold Bloom, Larzer Ziff, and Sacvan Bercovitch; some functioning both in and out of the academy, like Lionel Trilling and me. Thanks to them, certain hitherto underrated or ignored writers of the thirties—notably Nathanael West, Henry Roth, and Daniel Fuchs (all, by the way, Jews)—received their long overdue recognition, while simultaneously the overinflated reputations of other laureates of the Great Depression—James T. Farrell, for instance, John Steinbeck, and John Dos Passos (all goyim, to be sure)—were being deflated.

Such critics, moreover—especially as the English departments of major universities once closed to them opened up—eventually taught a new generation to read in new ways classic American writers like Hawthorne, Melville, and Whitman, as well as canonical modernists like Hemingway and Faulkner, Eliot and Pound, some of whom had themselves been anti-Semites, and all of whom had long remained the property of an exclusive WASP critical establishment. But our very success in this regard ended by dismaying me. Not only was I a little appalled by the fact that one by one even those among us who had been most ferociously anti-academic ended up with cushy academic appointments; I was even more dismayed at my own acceptance by a university system that had at first regarded me as an enemy in its camp. I was, to be sure, a little appalled when I—a Jew-boy from Newark, New Jersey—was invited to give the lecture at Bowdoin College honoring the 150th anniversary of Hawthorne's matriculation. But I was not truly unnerved until some years later I found myself at the University of Bologna as one of four Americans chosen to tell the Italians about American Puritanism and realized that all four of us were Jewish.

It was, I suppose, the equivalent in our little world of academia to the triumph in the larger world of culture represented by the granting of the Nobel Prize in Literature to Saul Bellow, followed shortly by the same award to Isaac Bashevis Singer. There is something, I could not help feeling, equivocal about that prize, which had, after all, been bestowed earlier on such a second-rater as Sinclair Lewis and such a nonentity as Pearl Buck. But, in any case, it has seemed to me always, whatever the merits of its recipient, somehow posthumous, marking the moment when a living author becomes a monument, a statue on a cenotaph. Certainly it marked the moment when Bellow, having become a subject for Ph. D. dissertations worldwide and seminars at the conventions of the Modern Language Association, belonged no longer to the outsiders, the beautiful losers.

But surely this was only to be expected, was it not (I admonished myself), since in our culture "nothing fails like success." And finally, as I had long been dimly aware, more particularly the very success of Jewish-American writers in thus becoming mouthpieces for all of America meant their disappearance as Jews, their assimilation into the anonymous mainstream of our culture. But was this not what we had been all the time wanting really, participants all of us, to one degree or another, in what has been called the "silent Holocaust"? Indeed, not a few of us had been only minimally Jewish to begin with, having long since abandoned the religion and even the cultural traditions of our ancestors. The awareness of this is, in fact, written into some of the key texts of the American-Jewish Renaissance; so that finally it seemed only just that in Saul Bellow's *The Dean's December* his protagonist and alter ego is presented not as a Jew but as a goy.

In any case, by the late sixties, though many of them continued to write and would for the next couple of decades, Jewish-American writers had ceased to seem central. This was due in part to certain political and social changes, to be sure. On the one hand, the Holocaust itself had faded from consciousness, particularly of the young; and some, indeed, not just lunatic-fringe fanatics but even a few respectable academics, began to question whether the slaughter of the Six Million had ever really occurred. Meanwhile, the State of Israel had come to seem no longer unequivocally heroic in its struggle against Arab terrorism, but more and more an oppressor of the Palestinians; so that on the New Left (though or because many of its most ardent adherents were themselves Jews) anti-Semitism reappeared in the guise of anti-Zionism, as it did, ever more virulently, in the black underclass and among the politicians, black and white, eager for those votes.

But there were esthetic as well as political reasons for the fall from favor of the Jewish-American novel, which began in the age of the counterculture. By the late sixties, Saul Bellow had come to seem to those of my students who, whatever their ideological bent, aspired to authorship, irrelevant, a belated nineteenth-century model committed to a brand of didactic realism that they found not just a dead-end but a bore. Though for a while I tried to argue them down, I found it harder and harder to remember, much less justify, my assertion not so many years before that Bellow was "perhaps of all our novelists the one we most need to understand, if we are to understand where the novel is going at the present moment."

Moreover, quite soon thereafter what we have come to call "postmodernist fiction" (I was, I feel obliged to confess, responsible for popularizing the use of that maddeningly ambiguous term) became the reigning genre and its authors were, as it turned out, chiefly gentiles. Yet it was the writers of such novels, chiefly John Hawkes and John Barth, whom at that period I read with most pleasure and touted most enthusiastically in print. In the years since, to be sure, they have not fulfilled all of my too euphoric expectations, but at least I keep thumbing through their latest books hopefully, as I have not done with the more recent novels of Malamud and Bellow and Roth. *Their* books continue to be read appreciatively, it is true, not just by dutiful scholars in quest of promotion and tenure, but by a general audience turned off, like those authors, by both the experimental metafictionists of the sixties and the goyish gurus of the age—Norman O. Brown, Marshall McLuhan, and Timothy Leary—who influenced them.

However ambivalently, I responded to those pagan prophets and the spirit of the time. Consequently, it was the rejection of that spirit and the consequent flight to gentility, academicism, and neoconservatism that motivated my split from the "New York intellectuals," with whom I had been for a long time quite unfairly linked. To be sure, I originally shared much with them, having grown up in an urban Jewish neighborhood from whose values I sought to escape by turning, on the one hand, to the literature of High Modernism and, on the other, to the writings of Marx, Lenin, and Trotsky. But, after all, I have never lived in New York—or, for that matter, in Chicago, Los Angeles, or San Francisco. Indeed, for twenty-three years at the very center of my life I was a citizen of Missoula, Montana, where I became not just a populist, but a *Western* populist, which is to say, a Westerner, and in some sense very nearly (I am not quite anything ever) a true melting-pot American. It is this, surely— along with a contempt for all canons, acquired by living through too many shifts of taste—that has led me to spend the last years of my life as a critic dealing with the Pop works that most ordinary Americans prize: Sherlock Holmes, Zane Grey, Edgar Rice Burroughs, and Margaret Mitchell. All of these are, of course, goyim; though they are also, of course, rejected by the high-toned goyish critical establishment as well as by the elitist Jews who aspire to that establishment.

In any case, by the late seventies I had announced publicly my divorce from the New York Jewish intellectuals and my resolve to write no more about their breakthrough into canonical culture. Not that I had exhausted the subject by any means. I had never, for instance, written at all about Jewish-American women writers like Grace Paley, Cynthia Ozick, Erica Jong, Esther Broner, or Rhoda Lerman, who had intrigued and moved me to a greater or lesser degree. Nor had I ever got around to an essay that I had long contemplated on James Baldwin and Ralph Ellison, two black writers who had first defined themselves and their themes for the overwhelmingly Jewish readers of *Commentary* and *Partisan Review*, and thus could be considered Jewish-American writers once removed. But I had come to feel that it was too late for either of these projects; that what I would write would be cued more by duty than by passion, and would therefore eventuate in instant clichés.

Nonetheless, when—approaching the terminal age of seventy —I began to gather together all my essays written over the previous couple of decades that I considered worth preserving, I discovered that there were enough on Jewish subjects to make a whole volume—the first of an intended three. That is to say, I found that no matter how far afield my new range of interests had taken me, I continued to write, willy-nilly, from a Jewish point of view, *as* a Jew. I had even, I was a little surprised to find, produced a belated essay or two on novelists of the Breakthrough about whom I had presumably said my last word. The first of these, called "The Many Names of S. Levin," represents my final backward glance at Bernard Malamud. This time, however, it was as a "Western" writer rather than as a Jewish one that I tried to come to terms with him, comparing his *A New Life* to Ken Kesey's *One Flew Over the Cuckoo's Nest*, which was not only set in the same part of the world but was published in the same year. In the second, I tried to make amends to Isaac Bashevis Singer for my long silence about his work, explaining the sense in which he was an emigré rather than an immigrant or child of immigrants—which is to say, an American-Jewish writer rather than a Jewish-American one, like Malamud or Bellow, who much admired him but whom he, apparently, has never read.

Moreover, though I write fewer and fewer book reviews these days (it is a form, I have come to feel, more appropriate for the tyro, the brash young man testing himself against the established old), those I have done turn out to be, like the pieces I have included on novels by William Styron, Norman Mailer, and James Atlas, occasions for reflecting on what Jewishness has come to mean at the end of the twentieth century. So, too, it was the problematics of contemporary Judaism that concerned me when I tried—also untypically—to do a proper academic study, returning to the Middle Ages, my first area of scholarly expertise. It was perhaps predictable that it would be the Grail legend that I dealt with in my last venture of that kind; and even more predictable that I would attempt to subvert the Christian-ness of that most Christian of myths by asking, "Why is the Grail Knight Jewish?" and, by implication, "Why was Chrétien de Troyes, who exploited it for anti-Semitic ends, Jewish as well?" I am not sure that I have answered either of those questions, or even that they are answerable. But merely to have posed them seemed to me sufficient—a way of paying off an old debt I did not even know I owed.

My interest in James Joyce, though it long remained amateur, extracurricular, predates even that in the Middle Ages. It began, in fact, with a present to me on my graduation from high school of the first edition of *Ulysses* legally permitted in the United States. The aunt who made me that gift in response to my relayed request had no way of knowing that what she was giving had long been labeled a "dirty book." Nor could she have foreseen that it was destined to become one of my all-time favorites, in part surely because I thought of it as forbidden rather than required like the OK literature we studied in English class. I have, indeed, read it more often than any other novel, with the exception of *Uncle Tom's Cabin* and *Huckleberry Finn*. Yet it was many years before I was willing to discuss it or its author before an academic audience, eventually appearing several times at symposia organized by the international James Joyce Society. Three of those lectures actually made it into print, but perhaps out of some vestigial reluctance to surrender my amateur status I did not include them in my *Collected Essays*. I cannot resist reprinting two of them, however, in this collection, since they make clear how in reading Joyce I have always identified with his comic, equivocally Jewish protagonist, Leopold Bloom—reading him, as a matter of fact, *as* Bloom.

The four remaining essays that constitute this volume were all originally composed in response to calls for me to testify on Jewish subjects as a representative, token Jew, as well as an American. I was, therefore, on each of these occasions, a Jew by definition even before I opened my mouth. I understood at long last what it really meant to be one of the Chosen People: to have no choice. The first of these, called "The Christian-ness of the Jewish-American Writer," I delivered in Jerusalem; the second, "The Roots of Anti-Semitism: A View from Italy," I presented in Florence. But the third and fourth, my meditations on the Book of Job and the two Holocausts, I wrote in the privacy of my own study at the behest of David Rosenberg, who had, he made clear, assumed that, like all the other contributors to his book, I am a Jew—whatever that means.

But "whatever that means" was precisely the question I could not help posing to myself as I was writing all four of these essays. I do not mean that I doubted for a moment (despite my rhetorical strategies in a couple of them) that I was in some ultimate sense a Jew; Hitler had decided that once and for all. I was, however, more and more confused about what a Jew is—in light of the fact that I can still call myself by that once tribal, sectarian name, though I have abandoned the traditional religion, almost completely lost the traditional culture and no longer speak the languages traditionally associated with Jewishness. I am consequently—as the volume in your hands tries to explain— a Jew only in retrospect, in memory; a memory that persists not in my heart or in my head but in my blood.

"In blood, in blood shalt thou remember," the *moel* intoned,

performing my circumcision; and it was not merely metaphorical blood he spilled. It is, therefore, in the actual blood that flows in my veins that I remember: an unbroken, unadulterated bloodline (I am convinced) going back through my working-class immigrant grandparents to the wonder-working rebbes of Galicia and ultimately to Aaron the High Priest himself. If I have been able to write these essays as a Jew, that is because, however problematical my relationship to my heritage in other respects, racially it is unequivocal. I am aware that these days both "blood" and "race" (thanks in large part to Hitler) have become taboo words, to be avoided by the enlightened and low-minded. But this does not trouble me a bit. Nor am I disturbed by the fact that the lineage to which I lay claim begins not with a man but with a myth. Such is the nature of all true high pedigrees, not least that of one with *chutzpah* enough to claim he is a Jew. *Whatever* that means.

Leslie A. Fiedler
Buffalo, New York
June, 1990

Fiedler on the Roof

The Roots of Anti-Semitism
A *View from Italy*

JUST after reaching seventy I found myself back in Italy, where I had first gone at precisely half that age, *nel mèzzo del cammin di nostra vita.* Small wonder I kept repeating to myself those opening words of *The Divine Comedy*, which I had been reading and rereading ever since my seventeenth year. "Midway in the journey of our life." I was half-convinced at that point that they were the charm that had brought me at the midpoint of my own life to Dante's native land; though I knew in fact that it was really the Fulbright Commission that had paid my way, so that I might talk about our books rather than theirs to Italian university students, who under fascism had been able to read them only behind the backs of their teachers. But this was only the prose truth, to which in 1952 I preferred the *bella menzógna*, the beautiful lie of poetry.

In 1987, however, I could find no appropriate verses to celebrate my return, which seemed to me not merely hopelessly prosaic, but disconcertingly anticlimactic, posthumous, as it were. After all, I had reached the end of my mythological life's journey of threescore years and ten. Nonetheless, my return to Italy seemed to me to deserve some sort of celebration, in prose at least if not in verse; because this time I was headed not for Rome or Venice or Bologna, where I had lived and lectured earlier, but for Florence, Dante's own city. Here I would at last make the sentimental pilgrimage I had long promised myself but somehow never accomplished to the Poet's house—and, especially, to the little church in which he had begun to dream his great poem, watching the head of his beloved Beatrice bowed in prayer.

It was, however, not as a *Dantista* that I had been invited back, nor even as an Americanist, expected to discuss Hawthorne and Melville, Mark Twain and Walt Whitman, but as a Jewish-American commentator on the plight of my people in multiethnic America. I could see no way out of that obligation, since the announced topic of the conference in which I had agreed to participate was—improbably enough, it seemed to me, conscious as I was of the fact that there were scarcely any Jews in Italy—"Jewishness and Anti-Semitism"; and—even more improbably—it had been organized by the Istituto Gramsci Toscano, which is to say, the Italian Communist Party. For Communists everywhere, I knew, the "Jewish Question" had always been more of an embarrassment than a central concern, so why had these Marxist-Leninists gathered, from a half-dozen countries, presumed experts on the subject, including—once more improbably—me? It did not take me long to realize, however, that the question answers itself. *Ubi morbus, ibi digitus* —where the itch is, there is the finger.

It was the bad conscience of the Italian Communists that explained it all: their nagging suspicion that their so-called "anti-Zionism," their flirtation with Qadaffi and the PLO, and especially the continuing harassment of refuseniks in the Soviet Union revealed, at the heart of their presumably "progressive" politics, the presence of the pathological hatred of Jews endemic in Western culture, pre-Christian, Christian, or post-Christian. Just as in the early days of the Church that primal phobia had been disguised in theological terms as "anti-Judaism," and in the heyday of the Enlightenment in pseudoanthropological ones about evolution and race, so from the beginnings of "scientific socialism" it was encoded in revolutionary "class-struggle" jargon, in which the Usurer who haunted the medieval imagination became the Capitalist, without ceasing to be the hawk-nosed perfidious Jew.

Nor did the identification of the Jew as class-enemy cease with the achievement of "Socialism in One Country" under Stalin. Indeed, it proved only too easy to replace the International Banker with the counterrevolutionary Trotsky-Bronstein: a mythological bugaboo as archetypally resonant as Judas, the Wandering Jew, Shylock, Fagin. Nor was Trotsky alone thus malignly mythicized—and eventually ritually executed. So also were Kamenev, Zinoviev, Radek, and other Old Bolsheviks, the Founding Fathers of the October Revolution, most of whom, it turned out, had been Jews—as the right-wing opponents of that Revolution, including Hitler himself, kept pointing out, thus disguising the anti-Semitism, which in fact they shared with the Communists, as anti-Communism.

Whether this strange fellowship embarrassed the anti-Communist Right I do not really know; but certainly it embarrassed the anti-fascist Left, and still does more than four decades after the downfall of the Third Reich. Why else did spokesmen for the Italian Communist Party keep rising in the midst of our symposium to intone like a litany of faith, "The Gulag is not Auschwitz. *The Gulag is not Auschwitz.*" I, at least, was not convinced. Nor did it help when those same apologists stopped arguing that the persecution of the Jews in the Soviet Union was not merely quantitatively but qualitatively different from that in Nazi Germany, seeking instead to dissociate themselves from their Russian counterparts. After all, they suggested, they were "Euro-Communists," with the accent on "Euro": the heirs not of Slavic barbarism but of Mediterranean civility, the High Culture of the Renaissance—of which the very city in which we met was a kind of living museum.

But how could we strangers from elsewhere forget this fact for a moment, since the municipal government of Florence (also Communist-controlled) had arranged for us to meet in the Palazzo Vecchio and the Medici Palace, through which even as our proceedings droned on tourists were tramping, along with hordes of noisy schoolchildren making required field trips to monuments of their country's glorious past. Moreover, lest all of this escape our notice, our sessions had been opened with a ceremonial fanfare played on antique trumpets by a half-dozen bored, middle-aged Florentines dressed in parti-colored Renaissance garb. All of this, however, seemed to me—as an American, a Jew, and a former ex-Stalinist—merely to compound the ironies implicit in the whole situation. Certainly, it confirmed me in my resolve to open my remarks by recounting how on one of my earliest trips to Italy (to which in the years between 1952 and 1987 I had become an almost regular commuter) I had been surprised to discover in the Ducal Palace at Urbino an anti-Semitic painting by Ucello called "The Desecration of the Host." Urbino, I had been taught in school, was, preceding even Florence, the birthplace of Renaissance culture; since it was there that Castiglione had written the first conduct book of the era, *Il Libro del Cortegiano*, even as his fellow-courtiers attempted to live out the genteel gentile role he defined. No one, however, had told me that, hung in honor on the walls of the palace of its reigning prince, was Ucello's baleful comic-strip sequence, whose first panel portrays a grossly caricatured Jew stabbing a consecrated wafer, which spurts blood under his knife; and whose final panel depicts that perfidious enemy of Christ apprehended and executed to the satisfaction of a crowd of gentile spectators—some of them clearly *cortegiani.*

What did *not* surprise me, however, was the knife in the hand of Ucello's stereotypical Jew, though such an icon has no source in the Christian scriptures. What inimical Jew, after all, wields such a weapon in the Gospel story? Not Judas. Not the High Priest. Not Barabbas, that dark double and antitype of Jesus, whose name means "the son of God." Not even the apocryphal mocker bid to "tarry till I come again." By then I had already begun to speculate on why, in certain classic English texts, embodying the indurated anti-Semitism of gentile Europe, the Jew appears thus armed. By 1949 I had even published a tentative, exploratory piece on the subject called "What Can We Do About Fagin?" But, dissatisfied with it, I have never republished it in any collection of my essays, though I have briefly developed some of its insights in my writing on other themes, particularly in the chapter on *The Merchant of Venice* in *The Stranger in Shakespeare.*

I suppose I always hoped that someday I would be able to finish that essay, but exactly when and how I was not sure, until I found myself so aptly back in Italy at twice thirty-five. It was only at that point I realized that to do the job right I would have to incorporate into my original piece the doubts that first assailed me in Urbino: doubts about whether assimilation into the traditional High Culture of the West did not mean for me —offspring of plebeian Eastern European Jews—a kind of apostasy, a falsification of my very identity. Yet it was my youthful desire to make that tradition my own, to become (there are no limits to the hubris of the young) its latter-day spokesman that had driven me to earn a Ph.D. in English literature and to come for the first time to Italy. Nor am I now prepared to abjure that tradition completely, despite the fact that I have come to feel my relationship to it ever more equivocal and problematic. I was in fact thrilled to be invited to return once more to Italy even by the Istituto Gramsci; and I must confess I found real pleasure in revisiting old scenes and old friends. Yet I have come, as I felt compelled to avow publicly in Florence, to feel less and less comfortable anywhere in Europe. Certainly I am not as ready as I once was to dismiss out of hand what my immigrant grandfather said to me (his words continue to ring like a reproach in my troubled head) when I told him I was about to sail back to the Jew-hating Old World which he had fled: "The dog returning to his vomit."

I find myself more and more these days, when my wanderlust recurs, inclined to travel instead to the Third World, to Latin America, Africa, the Orient, the Middle East—including Israel. But I have never on my brief visits to the homeland of my ancestors been tempted to take up permanent residence there, as I once teased myself with doing in Italy, since I feel myself more hopelessly a foreigner in Jerusalem and Tel Aviv and the Holy City of Safad than I do in Rome or Bologna or Florence. It is not merely that I can speak Italian better than Hebrew, which I scarcely know at all, or that long before I ever saw Italy I was familiar with its landscapes, its faces, its grandeur and squalor from a thousand well-loved pictures and books, but that Israel remains for me, even when I walk its streets, somehow an abstraction, a metaphor from a dull, half-forgotten sermon.

Even as in America I know I am a Jew and doubt that I am an American, in Zion (especially when some Orthodox zealot screams at me to put out my Sabbath Eve cigar) I know that I am an American and doubt that I am a Jew. Only in the land of Dante am I sure that I am both: a happy stranger in an amiable strange land, aware at every moment that I can and will return to my native land, where I will feel not at ease, as ill-befits a Jew, but at home: just one more exile in the midst of other exiles, rather than—like my forebears for all of their two thousand years in Europe—one of a barely tolerated rootless minority in the midst of a population whose roots go deep into the soil that Jews were not even permitted to till. It is our common revulsion from the values of that world that makes the most authentic American writers, WASPs that they are—Mark Twain, for instance, and Walt Whitman—seem spokesmen for my kind as well as theirs. "Sivilization" Twain calls that rejected European cultural inheritance; or rather he permits Huck Finn to use that pejorative, maliciously misspelled word at the moment he is about to "light out for the Territory ahead of the rest," meaning by "Territory" the westering edge of America, at a maximum distance from Europe and its influence. And Whitman makes explicit that it is not only the hierarchical class structures and limited freedoms of the Old World that he, like Twain, abjures, but Christian humanism itself. "Cross out please," he chants, inviting the Muse to migrate to America, "those immensely overpaid accounts,/ That matter of Troy and Achilles' wrath, and Aeneas', Odysseus' wanderings,/ Placard 'Removed' and 'To Let' on the rocks of your snowy Parnassus,/ Repeat at Jerusalem . . ."

It is perhaps for this reason that both of these masters of our demotic speech show no traces of anti-Semitism; though the same, alas, cannot be said of all American writers whom I have at one time or another immensely admired. Certainly it is not true of those High Modernist novelists and poets, from Henry James to Ezra Pound, T. S. Eliot to e. e. cummings, whom in my adolescence and early maturity I sought to emulate, feeling that only thus could I establish my credentials as a full-fledged, up-to-date citizen of the Republic of Letters.

Though I was until my middle twenties a Marxist as well as an aspiring author, I managed somehow to ignore the fact that most poets and novelists I sought to emulate were right-wing, some genteel conservatives, others hardcore fascists. Nor did it much trouble me (but why not? I ask myself now) that many of the "new poets" and experimental novelists I defended, in class and out, against their bourgeois, philistine detractors considered "Jews" the enemies of art, which is to say, bourgeois philistines par excellence. Such cultural anti-Semites included in their ranks not only the French *symbolistes* and the Italian futurists, to whom, after all, my affiliation was remote; even as it was to British writers like Wyndham Lewis and D. H. Lawrence, though the latter had settled briefly on our soil. But, more troublingly, their vilification of the Jews was echoed also by such American expatriates, self-made Europeans as T. S. Eliot and Ezra Pound, whom, throughout my long adolescence in Newark, New Jersey, I dreamed of following to the Old World.

I was able without much difficulty to dismiss their slanders of the people of Israel when it was confined to their obiter dicta, propagandistic essays in which I persuaded myself they falsified their authentic selves. Indeed, I forgot immediately after reading it Eliot's snide observation that no ideal society could "tolerate a large number of freethinking Jews"; nor did I linger long over Pound's hysterical insistence that the "higher kikery" had corrupted Western Christendom, whose champion was Mussolini. But what was I to do when I discovered similar slanders at the heart of their greatest poems, preserved still in present-day anthologies for classroom use, thanks in large part (it is a final irony) to a generation of Jewish critics and pedagogues—including me. Certain lines in their poems I could not then and still cannot read without wincing.

My house is a decayed house,
And the jew squats on the window sill, the owner,
Spawned in some estaminet of Antwerp . . .

The rats are underneath the piles.
The jew is underneath the lot.

Rachel *née* Rabinovitch
Tears at the grapes with murderous paws . . .

While I could still imagine no future American poetry not profoundly influenced by the example of Eliot—though some of it written, I dared hope, by Jews like me—I wrote to that aging poet, asking him about the obsessive hostility betrayed in such lines. I was expecting, I think, a recantation, an apology at least, since at the moment at which I opened our correspondence the full horror of the Holocaust had been revealed. He began in his response, by trying—rather unconvincingly, it seemed to me—to assure me that he was, of course, opposed to the Nazis' "Final Solution," that, indeed, he considered anti-Semitism a "heresy"; but he then went on to write, in a cliché almost as offensive as spelling the name of my people without a capital letter, that some of his best friends were Jews. And he concluded by unctuously expressing the hope that I was a faithful attendant of a synagogue in Missoula, Montana, which is to say, not, at least, "freethinking." But in Missoula there was no *shul* of any kind. Indeed, a minyan could not be assembled unless someone's relatives were visiting from elsewhere.

In any case, it scarcely mattered, I thought, crumpling up his letter and tossing it across the room, since what I mean by a Jew and he by a "jew" had nothing to do with organized religion. But this left me with the problem of puzzling out why, if not for having denied Jesus as the Christ, he hated the people who had. It was tempting to look for the roots of that hatred in his WASP ancestry, his class origins, his monarchist politics and, especially, his commitment to modernist esthetics. But none of these genetic theories would hold water, I finally decided; the same pathological response to Jews, believing or unbelieving, is also present in the books of other twentieth-century American writers, utterly different from him in race, class, and religious allegiance, including some who eschewed the pseudoclassicism of High Modernism. There was, for example, that mountain-boy, Thomas Wolfe, whose hawk-beaked Jewish businessmen, loud-mouthed Jewish students, and gross urban Jewesses with a taste for innocent gentiles from the sticks had made him a best-seller in Hitler's Germany; as well as that Midwestern offspring of non-English-speaking recent immigrants, Theodore Dreiser, who, despite his avowed atheism and long-term flirtation with the Stalinist Left, had also created nightmare travesties of the Jew as villain.

And finally there were F. Scott Fitzgerald and Ernest Hemingway, two of our most eminent modern novelists—rivaled only by William Faulkner. True enough, Fitzgerald had tried to make amends for his earlier anti-Semitism by creating, in his unfinished *The Last Tycoon*, the sympathetic Jewish character of Monroe Stahr. In his best-loved and most successful novel, *The Great Gatsby*, however, he reembodied all the most vicious anti-Semitic stereotypes of his time in the Jewish gangster, Wolfsheim, whose baleful, shadowy presence haunts the book from beginning to end. Wolfsheim is, to be sure, peripheral to the main plot; but Robert Cohn of Hemingway's *The Sun Also Rises* is not. Not merely is he central to the action of that novel, but, archetypal wimp that he is, against whom Hemingway's more admirable characters define their machismo and belongingness, he remains, alas, to this day the most vivid portrait of an American Jew in a book authored by a non-Jewish American.

As different as Fitzgerald and Hemingway are in other respects from James, Eliot, and Pound, however, there is one way in which they resembled them, being also Europe-oriented from the start, and for a while at least expatriates, seeking to redeem by returning to the Old World the provinciality of the land to which their ancestors had fled. True, Fitzgerald and Hemingway came home again; but they carried with them on their return a revived, renewed, exacerbated anti-Semitism, which—it can be argued—was a European import to begin with. God knows, certain forms of racism have been, if not invented, radically transformed in the United States: most notably, the miscegenation horror, which underlies the enslavement and subsequent discrimination against black Africans, and the fear and hatred of red-skinned Native Americans, which cued a three-hundred-year-long genocidal war against them.

But anti-Semitism was brought to our shores by refugee Europeans, at first largely Anglo-Saxon and Scotch-Irish, in whom it persisted undiminished even while there were so few actual Jews in the United States that most gentile Americans had never even seen one. It grew more virulent, however, when, during the last decades of the nineteenth century and the first of the twentieth, large numbers of Jews arrived on our shores, side by side with gentile immigrants from Southern and Eastern Europe. These latter-day, non-Jewish Americans did not have to learn anti-Semitic stereotypes from those who had arrived earlier, since they had already acquired them, both from folk tales and legends familiar even to the unlettered, and the High Culture of their countries of origin, wherever in Europe these might be. They had merely to translate them into English, or more precisely, I suppose, American.

Even now, moreover, the anti-Jewish prejudices they pass on to their children and children's children are reinforced from the same sources: from the story of "The Jew in the Bramble

Bush" for instance, in Grimm's *Fairy-Tales*, which they are encouraged to read in primary school; and from the "Great Books" of the Renaissance tradition from Chaucer to Shakespeare and beyond, which have been part of the required curriculum in English in the upper grades. To understand anti-Semitism in the New World, one must set it in the context of the Old World mythology implicit in such works, since the malign archetypal image of the Jew at their heart continues still to permeate the undermind of most Americans. In the forties and fifties of this century, I was convinced—over-impressed, I guess, by the wave of philo-Semitism that swept through my country, triggered by the shame and guilt following the full revelation of Nazi atrocities in the death camps—that this had all changed. And I was even more inclined to believe so when a generation of Jewish-American writers, including Saul Bellow, Bernard Malamud, Allen Ginsberg, Norman Mailer, and Joseph Heller were, so to speak, elected spokesmen to the nation, entrusted not only with creating new antimyths of the Jew, but with declaring to the entire world in their Jewish-American voices our common sense of who all of us, whether Jew or gentile, were or aspired to be.

The backlash against anti-Semitism apparently culminated in the recent twin awards of the Nobel Prize for Literature to Saul Bellow and Isaac Bashevis Singer. But as always such recognition proved to be retrospective—marking the end of the temporary domination of our culture by Jewish Americans. Certainly, neither Bellow nor Singer are the models for aspiring young writers in these "postmodern" times. It is, rather, goyim, neo-pagans like Donald Barthelme, John Barth, and Thomas Pynchon, who inspire novelists more interested in linguistic experimentation than exploring the human condition or the society around us. Moreover, contemporary authors still concerned with the victimization of the powerless deal with (and, indeed, tend to be) blacks, Native Americans, women, lesbians, gays, the disabled—anything but Jews.

In the political arena, it has also come to be considered unfashionable, or at least tactically inadvisable, to dwell on the plight of the survivors of Hitler, as was attested by the refusal of the delegates to the last national convention of the Democratic Party to take a strong stand against anti-Semitism, or even to condemn unequivocally anti-Semites like Louis Farrakhan and Jesse Jackson, who are both, of course, black. Reflecting on this fact, I realized, as I had not earlier, that the philo-Semitism of the forties and fifties had been confined almost entirely to the "progressive" white middle class. In the working class and the underclasses, particularly among blacks who had first learned it from their redneck Scotch-Irish neighbors in the South and relearned it from Eastern European ethnics, among whom they found themselves when they migrated to the cities of the East and Midwest, anti-Semitism never died. It only went underground for a while. But it emerged into full daylight, blatant and unashamed, even as the children of the white liberal bourgeoisie began to think of Jews not as the victims of Nazism, but as victimizers of the Palestinians, with whom—in their latter-day version of "progressivism"—even the Jews among them felt obliged to identify.

Finally, their parents, too, followed their example, or at least publicly pretended to do so. It is easy enough to think of political as well as family reasons for such accommodation on the part of those with political ambitions: a desire not to alienate the younger voters, for instance; or a resolve to maintain good relations with the oil-producing Arab nations, to whom Israel represents the intrusion of European *yids* into their ancestral homeland. Such specious and superficial explanations, however, although they explain the form that anti-Semitism takes at a particular place and historical moment, do not really illuminate the mystery of its persistence in a thousand different forms. To do so we must move beyond social or psychological analyses and ideological attempts to define the archetypal, the mythic underpinnings of a form of social paranoia that for millennia now has refused to die.

In light of the fact that anti-Semitism was until quite recent times absent from the non-Christian world (it never developed, for instance, in China or India), it can be argued that it is rooted in, inseparable from, the central myth of Christianity, the crucifixion of Christ at the instigation of the High Priests and with the assent of the people of Israel. My own first personal experience of gentile hostility would seem to confirm this: when I was perhaps seven or eight a gang of my fellow students chased me, the only Jew in our class, all the way home from school, screaming "You killed our Christ!" But though this assault by my peers left me baffled and in tears, it did not disturb me as much as being required a few years later to read *The Merchant of Venice*, and feeling the litany of abuse directed at Shylock, the Jew, aimed really (I was still the sole representative of my race present) at me.

What made matters worse was that by then I had begun to think of literature as a kind of sanctuary, an imaginary world in which I felt at home as I never did on the playground among jostling goyish jocks, or in weekly "chapel," where I sat in silence as everyone else recited the Lord's Prayer—*their* Lord's prayer. Listening, however, to my much-loved teacher prattle on about how this was a Christian play, preaching mercy as opposed to the rigor of Judaic law, I began to fear that not just Shakespeare's play but all the books we were taught as "our heritage" were—though in fact I responded to them more passionately than my gentile fellows—*theirs* too, which is to say, Christian and therefore necessarily anti-Semitic.

That Christians were not consistently anti-Semitic but only, as it were, by fits and starts, I should have realized even then, when long before I had forgotten it the kids who hunted me down as a Christ-killer elected me to class office. And that anti-Semitism was not unique to Christianity I could have learned from the Passover Haggadah, which teaches: "Not in one generation alone but in every generation they have risen up against us to destroy us . . ."; but in my "freethinking" household we never had a seder. I was, in any case, totally unprepared when years later the Roman Catholic Church officially absolved my people of deicide, and certain fundamentalist Protestant sects became the staunchest champions of Israel, leaving the persecution and killing of Jews to atheist "socialists" and orthodox Muslims, who also harried and slaughtered Christians. Moreover, in my own country, Christian prayer is now legally forbidden in the public schools, so that my children and grandchildren are spared having to sit through invocations to "Our Father . . ."

Nonetheless, it is hard for me to be at ease in the United States, as long as *The Merchant of Venice* is played and replayed on stage and screen and television and remains required reading in classes in English. Yet I have, in fact, recently assigned it to my own students. And how could I not? It is not only one of the most skillfully crafted of all Shakespeare's plays, but remains one of the most popular to this very day, and not just with avowed anti-Semites (Hitler loved it) but even with those convinced that they are free of the ethnic prejudices it exploits. But *why*? I ask myself and my students, each time I reread it, evoking once more the figure of Shylock as he was played on the Elizabethan stage, half-comic, half-horrific in his red wig and grotesque false nose.

Shylock, the Jew: that generic name is his real name, an epithet more insulting than any of the others directed at him —"dog," "wolf," "demon." But he has had, before and since Shakespeare, many aliases: Cartaphilus, Ahasuerus, Barabbas, Isaac of York, Fagin. Yet it is as "Shylock" that we remember him, because like many other characters in our literature, he has been baptized, "christened," once and for all, as it were, by Shakespeare. So, too, thanks once again to Shakespeare, we imagine him on the Rialto, though he has been reimagined in a score of other places, ranging from Constantinople and Malta to the underworld of London; and his true home is, of course, in the dreamworld of the gentiles, the nightmare from which they are still trying vainly to awake.

Out of their troubled sleep, he first emerged into written English literature in "The Prioress's Tale" of Chaucer, a poem extravagantly admired by his editors, one of whom praised it, unabashed by its virulent anti-Semitism, for its "artistic perfection" and "faultless beauty." That admiration, moreover, was shared by William Wordsworth, who produced a rather charming translation into modern English of the story, which had been many times told even before Chaucer. Some thirty earlier analogues have been discovered, and there existed, it would appear, a mystery play on the subject. But Chaucer altered the immemorial plot in two ways: first by making the child who is killed by the Jews much younger, a mere infant; and second, by eliminating the traditional happy ending of his miraculous resurrection. As Chaucer tells the tale, or rather lets his slightly ridiculous but essentially lovable Prioress tell it, it recounts how a boy so irked the usurious Jews of an unnamed Asiatic community that they hired a murderer to cut his throat and toss his body into a privy "where as the Iewes purgen her entraile." Though the boy is not finally brought back to life, the crime is revealed by a minor miracle, and its perpetrators are drawn and quartered, then hanged, as if to make doubly sure that they, too, stay dead.

From the start, three of the essential ingredients of the archetype I am exploring are present: the identification of the otherwise anonymous Jewish villains with usury, the knife as their chosen weapon, and a small male child as their victim— the latter two elements reminding us of an Old Testament episode, painted many times over in medieval and Renaissance times, which Christians insist on calling the Sacrifice (Jewish tradition refers to it rather as the Binding) of Isaac. So, too, Christian iconography portrays Isaac as a young boy, though the rabbis teach that he was thirty years old. At any rate, just such a bearded, patriarchal image of the Jew as infanticide has haunted the undermind of the West ever since, cueing, for instance, the scene in which Dickens portrays Fagin raising up against Oliver Twist a knife which, this time for once, does not fall. But, more insidiously, it has entered into actual history, breeding fantasies of the Passover sacrifice of gentile children, which have eventuated in bloody pogroms.

It was the report of a similar alleged atrocity, the crucifixion of little Hugh of Lincoln in 1255, an event memorialized in the Childe's Ballad called "The Jew's Daughter," that unleashed in England a wave of anti-Semitism, and was still on Chaucer's mind (he alludes to it in his final verses) when he wrote "The Prioress's Tale." So a similar outburst of lynch hysteria that was triggered by the trial of a converted Jewish court physician, accused falsely, as it turned out, though he was finally executed, of plotting to poison Queen Elizabeth, had repercussions on the literature of its time. At least three plays were written to provide vicarious release (there were almost no Jews on whom they could really vent it) for the audience's rage: Gosson's lost *The Jew*, Christopher Marlowe's *The Jew of Malta*, and Shakespeare's *The Merchant of Venice*. But Marlowe's Machiavellian

Jew lacks archetypal resonance, and is now known almost exclusively by scholars, while Gosson's survives only as an obscure reference in a dusty diary.

Shakespeare's Shylock, however, lives the immortal life of a true myth, appealing to the paranoia that persists, whether consciously or unconsciously, in the deep psyche of all gentiles—and stirring the corresponding fear of its consequences from which no Jew is ever quite free. In that character, whose very name is already mythic, Shakespeare not merely embodies all that so irked the Fathers of the Church: the Talmudic legalism and the stubborn refusal of the Jews to acknowledge the transfer of God's promise from them to the gentiles after their rejection of Christ. He attributes to him, also, a hostility to the secular values of European feudal aristocracy, making him a hater of music, a distruster of courtly love, an enemy of the pleasure principle. And finally, of course, he portrays him as an advocate of usury, which challenges both. He is more, though, than the familiar money-grabber with a knife, because for the first time his vendetta against the gentile world and his lust for revenge is associated with the "merry bond" and the "pound of flesh." Shakespeare, to be sure, did not invent these motifs, which had in fact appeared fairly often in earlier folktales, in some of which the proposer of the bloody pact was already identified as a Jew.

Only in *The Merchant of Venice*, however, are they combined with the other elements that together constitute the mythic substrate of European anti-Semitism: the archetypal tale of Abraham and Isaac. Twice that patriarch (whose name fittingly enough is always on Shylock's lips) is described in the scriptural account as raising a threatening blade against his son: once for his sacrifice, from which he escapes unscathed; and once for his circumcision, in which his blood is actually drawn. But in Hebrew the word for circumcision is *brith*, meaning the covenant, the bond; what is memorialized in the rite ("In blood, in blood shalt thou remember," its celebrant intones) is God's contractual promise to the Father of Israel that his seed will be chosen over all the peoples of the earth.

In the undermind of gentile Europe, the aborted sacrifice and the accomplished excision of the foreskin (disavowing which early Christianity ceased to be a Jewish sect and became a rival religion) tend to blur into a nightmare of threatened castration. This is made manifest in Shakespeare's play, where the intended victim of the Jewish father's knife is no longer—as in Chaucer—a boy-child but an adult male. Antonio is, in its climactic scene, stripped as if for a sacrifice; and though it is stipulated in the "merry bond" that the "pound of flesh" (the ante has been raised considerably) is to be cut from an area "nearest the merchant's heart," this seems an obvious displacement upward from the genitals, for a marriage is at stake, *three* marriages in fact, which is to say that what the Jew's blade finally threatens is love and fertility.

There is a sense in which the paranoid castration fear embodied in the myth of Shylock tells a kind of truth, as is scarcely surprising in light of the fact that—as Freud was once moved to observe—the paranoiac never lies. Judaism did indeed threaten to unman the gentile world, insofar as Jewish morality, transmitted via Christianity, sought to limit and control the "free" sexuality presumably enjoyed by males in pre-Christian Europe. To the degree, then, that masculine Europe has remained pagan in its deep psyche, it imagines that morality holding a knife to its genitals. The resentment engendered by such fantasies is, of course, really directed against the Church and its teachings; but believing Christians have felt it impossible to confess this. Instead, they project it backward onto the Jewish patriarch Abraham.

Abraham, however, is the founding father of Christianity as

well as Judaism, from which indeed the later faith springs. To symbolize that somewhat embarrassing affiliation (thus also disguising the anti-Christianity implicit in anti-Semitism), Shakespeare created in Jessica the figure of the bad Jew's good daughter, who, even as her evil progenitor vanishes from the scene, ends up "happily ever after" in the arms of a gentile bridegroom. There had been other Jew's daughters in English literature long before Jessica; but the first of them all, who appears in the Ballad about Hugh of Lincoln, is portrayed as being as malign as her father: a willing accomplice in the plot to lure a gentile victim to his doom. Though the Abigail of Marlowe's *The Jew of Malta* seems at the play's start to be such a dark temptress, she turns in the end benign, which is to say, a friend to the Christians as well as an enemy to her father.

It is not until *The Merchant of Venice*, however, that the figure of the Jew's daughter achieves her full archetypal significance. From that point on, indeed, she functions as a true myth, embodied over and over in later literature—as the Rebecca, for instance, of Sir Walter Scott's *Ivanhoe* and the Ruth of Herman Melville's *Clarel*. But what is signified by this archetype? To answer that question, one need only reflect on the fact that even as in the popular imagination of gentile Europe the first of the Hebrew patriarchs had somehow come to be regarded as malign, Mary, the Mother of the Redeemer, continued to be thought of as a Jewess, which is to say, his daughter. In the story of Shylock and Jessica, that double vision, with its attendant ambivalence toward the Jews, is archetypally embodied. Moreover, Shylock as the evil, forbidding father of a desirable girl fades into the fairy-tale figure of the ogre, more beast than human, from whom the hero can steal both his daughter and his treasure (somehow symbolic equivalents) without compunction or guilt.

To make clear his bestial nature, Shakespeare has other characters describe the evil Jewish father in animal terms:

> O be thou damned, inexecrable dogge . . .
> Thou almost mak'st me waver in my faith,
> To hold the opinion with Pythagoras
> That soules of Animals infuse themselves
> Into the trunks of men. Thy currish spirit
> Governed a Wolfe . . .

In Pope's *Moral Essays* the toad, more horrific for not being specifically named, is substituted for the dog, which had risen in social esteem between Shakespeare's age and his:

> And every child hates Shylock, though his soul
> Still sits at squat, and peeps not from its hole . . .

And the suggestion is echoed in Eliot's line about the "jew" who "squats on the window sill, the owner . . ." True enough, in Eliot's case (in this sense his response to me contained a grain of truth) the myth of the bestial Jew is no longer associated with the lynch spirit to which Chaucer's poem and Shakespeare's play responded. It reflects, like the casual anti-Semitic remarks in the popular literature of our time (I think, in particular, of Graham Greene and Agatha Christie), an irrepressible vestigial shudder rather than the lust for a pogrom, a feeling nowhere better described than in an essay by William Hazlitt called "On the Pleasure of Hating":

> A child, a woman, a clown, or a moralist a century
> ago would have crushed the little reptile to death—
> my philosophy has got beyond that—I bear the crea-

ture no ill will, but still I hate the very sight of it. . . .
We give up the external demonstration, the *brute*
violence, but cannot part with the essence or principle of hostility. We do not tread upon the poor
little animal in question (that seems barbarous and
pitiful!) but we regard it with a sort of mystic horror
and superstitious loathing. It will ask another
hundred years of fine writing and hard thinking to
cure us of the prejudice, and make us feel towards
this ill-omened tribe with something of "the milk of
human kindness," instead of their own shyness and
venom.

These lines were written of *spiders*, but with scarcely a change
they can be read, alas (as I first read them), as referring to Jews.
Jews, however, are thinking spiders, vermin that walk like men.
Before the Enlightenment, though, our ill-omened tribe lived
in a world as remote from the world of Western culture as an
insect society, so that if we were not actually stepped on, we
did not suffer. But now we are troubled by the most casual anti-
Semitic slur in the books of that culture to which we have sought
to assimilate. We buy them, read them, are hurt by them,
terrified by them, for whatever a hundred years of "fine writing
and hard thinking" has done for the spiders, it has brought us
Hitler. Consequently, Hazlitt's pious belief that even by his
time "superstitious loathing" was severed forever from overt
violence seems to us dubious at best. Where, then, do we, as
reasoning reptiles, go from here? What response can—*should*
—we make to a culture in which so terrible and perilous a myth
of ourselves is inextricably rooted?

We could, I suppose, solve the whole problem by pulling back
into a cultural ghetto, where only sticks and stones can break

our bones. Perhaps, after all, it is time to admit after two hundred years that our attempt to assimilate to Western "civilization" has been a mistake and to seek refuge, as some have done in Israel, or to retreat, like others, to the closed community of Hasidic Orthodoxy. But I, at least, cannot help feeling that we have given too many hostages to the West, so that fleeing it we would be forced to leave behind our Montaignes and Spinozas, our Prousts and Freuds, our Einsteins and Kafkas, our Blochs and Soutines, not to mention our homegrown Nathanael Wests, Henry Roths, Saul Bellows, and Bernard Malamuds.

To those who feel as I do in this respect (particularly if they be scholars and pedagogues) a preferable alternative seems the "kidnapping" of the very myths that exclude us, by reading into them more sympathetic meanings. So certain of my colleagues have attempted to reinterpret *The Merchant of Venice*, convinced apparently that if only it were redeemed from the anti-Semites, all would be solved. For a hundred years now the manifest anti-Semitic intent of Shakespeare's play has been explained away by good-hearted commentators; one of them argued recently, for instance, that "Shakespeare rarely 'takes sides' and it is certainly rash to assume that he here takes an unambiguous stand 'for' Antonio and 'against' Shylock. . . ." A more effective attack, however, has been launched in the theater, where since the mid-nineteenth century the tradition of acting Shylock as a tragic and suffering victim has replaced the original portrayal of him as a burlesqued villain—the *"oi! oi! oi!"* interpretation, which apparently had them rolling in the aisles at the Globe.

Heine writes in 1856 of having seen such a euphemizing production in Drury Lane, at which a "pale, fair Briton" was moved to weep and cry out of Shylock, "The poor man is wronged." But there is an underlying note of hostility toward

Jews in the play that cannot be thus sentimentalized out of existence; so that writing at almost the same moment, another German critic, returning from a performance, was moved to jot down the terrible words of Luther, confirmed, he felt, by Shylock's behavior: "Know then, dear Christian, that, next to the Devil, thou canst have no bitterer, fiercer foe than a genuine Jew, one who is Jew in earnest. The true counsel I give thee, is that fire be put to their synagogues, and that, over what will not burn up, the earth be heaped and piled, so that no stone or trace of them be seen for evermore."

Such appropriation of myth alters, in any event, only our conscious responses. Whenever, therefore, *The Merchant of Venice* is played, there is a risk of its stirring to life in the beholder a fear and hatred of "the Jew" not only older than any recent "humane" interpretation, but older than the dramatic form in which Shakespeare cast it. For this reason, in recent years there have been many attempts by Jews, enjoying economic, social, and political freedom in the West, to eliminate what they feel to be their last remaining indignity by expurgating the culture into which they have so successfully assimilated. Pickets have marched before a movie version of *Oliver Twist*; "The Prioress's Tale" has been, under pressure, omitted from a new translation of Chaucer into modern English; and proposals have been made to remove both *Ivanhoe* and—of course, of course—*The Merchant of Venice* from required reading lists in public schools. In this attempt to keep their own children from reading Shakespeare's great play, American Jews have gone even further than their brethren in Israel, who forbid it only to Arab students on the West Bank.

At least we have not yet in our righteous indignation felt impelled to make bonfires out of such offensive literature. But even if every last copy of *The Merchant of Venice* were burned to ashes, what would we have accomplished beyond symbolically destroying some printed texts in which a sixteenth-century English poet incarnated for his time and place an all but immortal archetype? The myth of Shylock may indeed die, as all myths eventually die when they no longer serve psychosocial needs; but it cannot be killed. In attempting to kill it, moreover, we not merely yield to hysteria in ourselves, but risk unleashing a counterhysteria in others, of which we would ourselves be victims. In light of our long troubled history, it seems clearly absurd for Jews to become censors, or for the People of the Book to prepare a latter-day index of forbidden literature.

In any case, aware of how I, and indeed all Jews, have benefited from the protection of the First Amendment, I am willing to defend against book-banners even bad writers, whose values I myself consider vicious; including not just sadomasochists and hard-core pornographers, but anti-Semites as well. All the more, then, am I prepared to defend those works of Shakespeare or Dickens or Pound, in which anti-Semitism is rendered with elegance and wit. It is, moreover, my profoundest belief that it is better for the gentiles to indulge that dark passion vicariously, symbolically (thus, perhaps, finally exorcizing it) rather than to let it fester unconfessed in the dark underside of their psyches, until it explodes in overt violence.

If, however, *The Merchant of Venice* is to have such a cathartic effect, its readers and beholders must acknowledge that the evil embodied in Shylock, his avarice, pride, distrust of pleasure, even the desire to mutilate what he hates, is present to some degree in all of us—not, of course, as we are Jews *or* gentiles, but only as we are humans. This, in fact, I knew before I had ever read Shakespeare; I had first heard the story of the pound of flesh from my grandfather, who had, I suppose, heard it from his. In his version, at any rate, the fatal confrontation

in the courtroom was not between a good Christian and a bad
Jew, but between a good Jew and a bad, which is to say, between
people quite like us on both sides.

Yet this did not keep me from wincing (as I have already
confessed), when I encountered Shylock in print. Indeed, I will
continue to do so, I am sure, until the gentiles have learned to
wince for having thus identified moral obliquity exclusively with
us. Nor can we Jews hasten the process by protesting or preaching. They must themselves come to realize that Shylock is the
product of their guilt and fear, a stratagem for projecting what
they must needs recognize as evil in themselves onto an alien
Other. Already there are signs that such a recognition has begun, but not everywhere in the world—not even everywhere
in America. And this troubles me deeply.

Not that I expect here in the United States (despite some
muttering from disaffected blacks, and shouting of hostile slo-
gans on the pro-Palestinian Left or the neo-Nazi Right) organized pogroms or even widespread discrimination. In the
foreseeable future, I am quite convinced, American Jews will
live, as I have come to live, at peace with their neighbors as
their forebears in the Old World never were; and many of them
will, as some of them already have, grow prosperous to a degree
that those forebears did not even dare to dream. Nonetheless,
our children and our children's children will continue to be
required to read or compelled to look at books and pictures
embodying the anti-Semitic myths of the Old World. And how,
after the experience of Hitlerism, is it possible not to be aware
that even smoldering ashes of those myths can be blown into
flame when will and circumstance conspire?

What, then, can be done to ensure against such an event by
Jewish-American artists and intellectuals, still committed in the
dying twentieth century to a culture of whose dangers they are
only too well aware? Little more, I fear, than has been done

already by the generation of Jewish-American writers who came of age after World War II, and for a little while at least captured the imagination of gentiles not just in their own country but throughout the world. Such novelists and poets sought to fight fire with fire, as it were—adopting the language and conventions of a culture that regarded them as alien to create rival myths of the Jew, characters of archetypal resonance like Malamud's Fidelman, Roth's Portnoy, and especially Bellow's Herzog and Augie March.

Meanwhile, I, of the same generation, have as a critic attempted to create a therapeutic Jewish metamyth of mythic anti-Semitism; and though, to be sure, we have not succeeded in exorcising anti-Semitism from the underminds of our gentile neighbors or the fear of it from our own, we have, I think, made a difference. It is not merely that we have altered the cadences of American speech and the manners of the American academy, for better or for worse; but that since our large-scale incursion into its very heart, Western culture as a whole, which was being Americanized even as America was becoming Judaized, will never be the same. And that, from our point of view, can only be an improvement.

Bloom on Joyce; or
Jokey for Jacob

I INTEND to speak to you tonight not about Bloom, but *as* Bloom, in part because I have been listening for several days now to what seems to me to have been too exclusively the voice of the half of Joyce that is Stephen Dedalus; or rather the voice of a kind of sub-Stephen or post-Stephen, which is to say, the voice of Stephen Dedalus, Ph.D.

But I rise before you in the guise of Bloom, who could never have a Ph.D. or M.A. or even B.A., in part also because it is, after all—sixty-five years after the event—Bloom's day again, and not only Bloomsday, but Bloom's hour. We have it on the very best authority that "as the day wears on, Bloom should overshadow them all." But seven days have worn on, in fact, from dawn to dark, and it's now time, and more than time, for Bloom. Finally, however, I have assumed and am assuming at this moment the voice of Bloom because it is the voice of the eternal amateur, the self-appointed prophet, the harassed Jew, the comic father; and that is a voice which I like to believe, for my own private reasons and some public ones too, is my own authentic voice. And I am resolved to speak to you today in the most authentic voice I can find, as personally and nonprofessionally as I can manage, because I would be a little embarrassed in rising before you otherwise, since I can claim absolutely no expertise in Joycean matters. To speak, therefore, to the experts who are gathered here on any other terms except the terms of an amateur would be, as the Chinese say, to peddle books before the door of Confucius.

Let me begin, then, by declaring as confessionally and personally as I can that not only am I somebody who has read almost nothing of Joyce scholarship, which I suspect (unfairly I have no doubt) of being a purgatorial mountain, crowned not with an earthly paradise but a desert; but that also I have read very little of the very little that can be called properly Joyce literary criticism. My credentials for accepting your kind invitation to speak to you on this occasion at the very end of your long series of meetings are only that for some thirty-five years now, which is a long enough time in good faith, I have read and re-read, remembered and re-remembered, loved and hated, *lived*, I think I can fairly say, the works of James Joyce. I remember very clearly, as I stand here years later, the moment when I begged and bullied and wheedled (I was I think about fourteen or fifteen years old) a copy of *A Portrait of the Artist* out of the locked room of our local library, where it had been hidden away, as is proper with obscene literature, from the young and susceptible. And I remember even more clearly the year I was seventeen and Judge Woolsey's decision had just released *Ulysses* from the underground to the above-ground circulation. And I can remember most clearly of all the moment I was given a copy of *Ulysses* as a high school graduation present by a very genteel aunt who would have been shocked out of her small mind if she had realized what she was putting into my hands. I remember, finally, the sixty days just before the landing of the American troops on Iwo Jima, when under fire and all at sea, which seems a perfect symbolical situation for reading *Finnegans Wake*, I read through *Finnegans Wake* for the first time.

What I am trying to say to you is that I have been living Joyce for a long time now, and especially I have been living *Ulysses*, not outside of but within the very texture of my life, as a part of the process of growing up and growing old. *Ulysses* was for my youth and has remained for my later years not a novel at all, but a conduct book, a guide to salvation through the mode of art, a kind of secular scripture. Yet I, who have written about almost everything in the world that has crossed my desk or entered my head, am pleased to tell you that I have never written a word about *Ulysses*—not a single word. I have never, as they say, taught *Ulysses*—talked about it in class. I have never spoken in public about *Ulysses* before, though I am, as some of you may know, a garrulous man, reticent about almost nothing, and I have become more and more a public man given to talking about the things that most intimately concern me to any random audience that will pause to listen.

Until tonight I have kept silence on the subject of my own relationship to Joyce, and especially to *Ulysses*, as if somehow it was too dear and dirty, too—in the full Joycean sense of the word—"holy," to discuss in a profane situation and circumstance. But, as you are all surely aware at this point, I have been unable to resist the temptation to speak out at last, here and now; which is to say, as the sacred day wears itself to a close, and I am privileged to rise in that Dublin which has existed in my head for a long time, and in which I find it very hard to believe I am at last existing in the flesh. If I had been born on the first day that I read *Ulysses*, it occurs to me, and in some sense I was born on that day, I would now be, and in some sense I am, precisely in the middle of the journey of our life. Time enough, then, to say my word.

But I have been discovering that at a point when I am finally ready to speak about Joyce and *Ulysses*, it may turn out that I have waited too long; that it may, in fact, be, if not quite too late for me, for anyone, to declare his love for *Ulysses* and his debt to Joyce, very nearly too late to do so. Let me be as candid as I can on this score. I have in the past several years become more and more aware, painfully aware, that the literary movement we have agreed to call "modernism," and at the center of which Joyce stands, is a literary movement which is now dead. We live, that is to say, at a moment when modernism is no longer viable for young writers and readers, or even for what is young and living in old writers and readers. I am kept especially uncomfortably aware of this fact by those who deny it: the embalmers of modernism, those scholars who seek through pedantry and patience, the undertaker's art, to forge a living smile on the face of a corpse.

It distresses me deeply to realize that Proust, Mann, and Joyce no longer seem the names of three exciting and dangerous authors, but a title of a standard course in college curricula all up and down the United States. And in this postmodernist era, it is very easy to perceive, and hard not to be overimpressed by, the limitations of modernism, which suddenly become as clear to us as the virtues of that movement once were.

It seems to me, at any rate, that the age of the art novel and the culture religion is over: that age so utterly lost in elitism and snobbism, the vestiges of class values totally alien to a democratic or mass society, that it was doomed from the first to die the academic death. The very notion of avant-garde, which haunted Joyce and his contemporaries, with its dream of taking by storm the libraries and classrooms of the future, strikes me now as having been in every sense a dead end. And I find myself repelled a little as I look back at those young surrogates of their authors who live at the center of certain "avant-garde" masterpieces, of whom Stephen is the epitome and archetype: those miserable creatures who chose to go through and even into Hell—not like Dante, in order to save themselves, or like Huck Finn to save someone they loved—but only so that after they return they can write books about what it was like to be there—thus ensuring themselves posthumous fame. But though highbrow critics may have been taken in by this strategy, the popular audience has not.

I've been moved and troubled, for instance, by the still evident disaffection of the Irish themselves from Joyce, of which I have been reminded by the people of Dublin, as willing to talk about this as about anything they have on their minds. And I have come to the conclusion that the disaffection they register (let us be truthful with ourselves on this score) is neither accidental or incidental, nor is it, as I once would have believed, a necessary adjunct of greatness. To be great is not, I now believe, necessarily to be misunderstood.

The Irish people have managed somehow to accept their other great artists and disturbers of the peace, all the way from Yeats to Brendan Behan, but not Joyce. No, I am convinced that the fate of Joyce, the special exclusion of Joyce from the hearts of his people, is a fate he deliberately sought, misguidedly, I now believe, and foolishly, cripplingly. It is a fate Joyce *chose*, not endured. Typical in this regard (and if I refer to this with special passion, it is because it's a subject that especially moves me) is Joyce's mode of handling myth. Unlike those writers who close rather than widen the gap between the elite audience and the great audience, between high art and popular art, Joyce tends most of the time not to create or to release or to evoke new myths, a new mythology, a reborn mythology, a resurrected

mythology; but rather to reinterpret old and dying myths, or
to dissolve them in irony, or, worst of all, to move them closer
and closer to the level of total abstraction. His powers, I am
trying to suggest, seem to me a good deal of the time mytho-
graphic rather than truly mythopoeic and mythoplastic. He is
less a dreamer of dreams than an interpreter of dreams. And
the art of myth criticism, which is the essential art of a great
deal of Joyce, as it is also of other modernist works like Mann's
Joseph tetralogy or *The Waste Land* of T. S. Eliot, takes us not
to the place where we are one with each other—whether we
are born Nora Joyce or James Joyce—but to a place where we
are aware of our differences from each other and we are
tempted, respectively, on the Nora side and the James side, to
condescension and *ressentiment*.

Let me be very personal about this. I don't want to sound as
if I'm talking abstractly about something that applies to somebody else rather than to me. And even if I cannot be quite as
candid as I have pledged to myself to be, at least let me be as
candid as I can manage to be on such an occasion. How clear
it seems to me now that my own first relationship to Joyce, my
own first uses of James Joyce, which were essentially a relationship to and uses of the figure of the insufferable Stephen,
were more ignoble than I could then have believed or than I
now like to confess.

He fit only too well my young man's desire to make it into a
world that excluded me by proving myself in possession of a
work too difficult to be available to others; my young man's
impulse to culture-climb to a place where I could be at one and
the same time an alienated artist, much loved for that very
alienation by a substantial minority audience, and a Ph.D.,
immune to the stuffiness of all other Ph.D.'s though just as job-
secure as anybody else in the university system. What a foolish
illusion it was; what a lovely illusion it was; what an irresistibly

lovely foolish illusion it was: to win acclaim and academic promotion by parsing the satanic slogan, *non serviam*, or by teaching young people to repeat it after me in class for grades.

I don't want to load all my own petty sins on Joyce, and I'm
trying very hard not to do this; since there's small point in using
an occasion like this to turn Joyce into some sort of symposium
scapegoat to be sent back out into the academic desert from
which we have all come, with all our outgrown sins on his back.
It's not a desire for self-exculpation, but a longing for uncus-
tomary frankness which prompts me to insist that part of the
fault for the sins which were truly mine was, in fact, Joyce's.

Some of you here before me were present, I know, at the
Bailey early in the symposium, early in this conference week,
when a young man arose suddenly, looking like a reborn,
younger version of the Citizen in the Cyclops episode, to shout
at a group of us happy Stephens gathered around him, "I am
an illegitimate grandson of James Joyce, and I want to tell you
that he would *spit* on every one of you." Ah, the young man
was wrong, alas, since I fear that Joyce would have approved
rather than spit upon even what is the worst about us and our
deliberations. He would have loved all of us factification-forgers
and exagmination-makers. He would have relished the endless
pilpul, the Talmudic exegesis, in which the sacred is profaned
without any feelings of guilt. He would have rejoiced, after all,
at the soulless industry that has grown up around his tortured
and obsessive works. "God have mercy on his soul and what
remains of ours." This is my prayer for the night.

Having said all this, I am obviously obliged to ask, along with
you who have hopefully listened to it all, the question: "Is there
nothing then left for me to celebrate on Bloomsday? Is there
nothing left for me to celebrate on this night, in this place? I
who believe that literature should be not *about* myth but living
myth itself. I who have lost my taste for the ironic and have

grown perhaps overfond of the comic and the pathetic. I who believe that criticism itself, which is a form of literature and not of science, should aim not at exagmination but at ecstasis.

And the answer is yes—yes, yes, *yes*. There is much to celebrate on Bloomsday, and that much bears the name of Bloom himself. On Bloomsday we can celebrate Bloom: not merely the archetypal character called by that name, but everything in the whole corpus of Joyce's works that is written by Bloom-Joyce rather than by Stephen-Joyce; by a Jew-Joyce rather than by the first-martyr-to-the-Jews Joyce. And when I say that Bloom remains to celebrate that is a way of telling you that virtually *everything* remains to celebrate, since all the rest is nothing.

Bloom himself is not merely mythic, much less an ironic commentary on a dying myth. He is a true, a full myth, a new and living myth. He is, to be sure, based on—reflects off of—the figure of Homer's Ulysses, that Greek version of, as Joyce liked to believe and I'm prepared to believe with him, a Semitic prototype. But Bloom is Ulysses resurrected and transfigured, not merely recalled or commented on or explained. Bloom is Ulysses rescued from all those others who were neither Jew nor Greek, and who had kidnapped him, held him in alien captivity for too long. Bloom is Ulysses rescued from the great poets as well as the small ones, from Dante and from Tennyson, and—at the other end of the mythological spectrum from James Joyce—from that anti-Semite, Ezra Pound, who liked to think he was the only true Ulysses.

In fact, however, Ulysses, the old Ulysses, the remembered Ulysses, the re-evoked Ulysses, constitutes only a small part of the total Bloom, the part that the Stephen in Joyce, everything in him that was not Bloom, could most easily deal with, *had* to deal with in order to keep the tidy schematic structure, which he unwisely loved, and to plant clues for future exegetes whom he unfortunately desired.

The larger part of Bloom came not from memories of Homer's Ulysses, and not from the top of the head of Joyce, the name for which is Stephen. No, much, perhaps most, of what constitutes the authentic figure of Bloom comes, perhaps not entirely unbidden and unconsciously, but certainly less cerebrally, from deeper, darker, more visceral sources. The myth of Ulysses lives in the head of Christian Europe, but the myth of the Jew, which is Bloom's better half, resides in the guts of Europe: a pain in the dark innards of the gentile world, or better perhaps, an ache in the genitals, an ache in the loins of the gentiles.

Remember, please, for a minute with me what is hard for me to remember, easy for me to forget. How unprecedented, how radically new, Joyce's Jew was in the dark world of Christian mythology about Jews. To be sure, there had been a gentile writer, or two or three, before Joyce who had tried to evoke a benign, a blessed, a favorable image of the Jew: George Eliot, for instance, in that oddly hermaphroditic figure of Daniel Deronda; or Dickens in the quite unbelievable portrait of the sickly, sweet, and sentimental Riah.

But essentially the troubled sleep of a Europe still pagan at the moment Joyce began to write his book was haunted by the figure of the Jew as a wicked and destructive father with a knife in his hand, Shylock or Fagin or those attenuated mythological descendants of Shylock and Fagin who persist in Joyce's contemporaries like T. S. Eliot and Ezra Pound. One is tempted to say that insofar as the mind of Christianity continued to contemplate, to try to assimilate, a Christianity it secretly resented, the mind, the mind of gentile Europe, was destined to hate and vilify the Jews who had imposed upon it the burden of a religion with which it could never come to terms.

This is the meaning, a meaning of the figure of Father Abraham, isn't it, after all? That prototypical Jewish father, distorted, by the bad dreams that possess the undermind of Europe, into an image of terror, in which the double indignity visited upon the son, the eternal Isaac, becomes one: the circumcision that was actually performed, and the aborted ritual sacrifice blended into the single threat of castration. And surely behind the quarrel of Christian Europe with the first patriarch of the Jews, there lurks a deeper, less confessable uneasiness with that more ultimate Father who ordered the circumcision and the sacrifice, with the God of Abraham, Isaac, Jacob, and Joseph, whom the converted pagans of Europe cannot help feeling somehow took away their primitive manhood, their genital power, by making them all in some symbolic sense eunuchs for the sake of the Kingdom of Heaven.

But in Joyce, and in him for the first time, the Jew, though he remains a father still, is no longer a dark, threatening, castrating father. He is no threat to anyone, because he is no longer Abraham, but Joseph: Joseph the carpenter, Joseph the joiner, which is to say, he is the cuckold, since for Joyce there is no Christian-Jewish God anymore. And in a world where old Nobodaddy is dead, we are all the sons not of even Abraham, much less of Abraham's God, but only of the carpenter-cuckold, the comic old artificer, who is really closer to the limping, laughable figure of Hephaestus, the husband of Aphrodite, than to Ulysses, who, after all, drew a bow that no rival suitor could manage. It's the comic unmanned father we can manage to love, the unfeared father; and Joyce has given us an enduring image for that blessed, ridiculous archetypal parent, an image appropriate to the early twentieth century, appropriate to us still as that century draws to a close.

Bloom, however, does not stand alone, for there is a whole company, you know, of such impotent Good Father figures: Falstaff and Nigger Jim and Pickwick, and God only knows who else. But it is the distinction of Bloom to be the sole Jew in that comic, harmless, beautiful company. And to be a Jew, moreover, who was invented by, dreamed out of himself, separated from his own body in sleep, by an Irishman—an Irish Jew imagined by an Irish poet, who, in a world without gods or goddesses, felt obliged to be his own God as well as his own Muse.

This is what finally intrigues me, what finally I want to talk to you about: this last, best joke of all, this kind of joke on a joke, this ultimate comic turn of the screw, the delicious fact that the great good Jewish father of the modern world was invented by an Irishman. You know, just to say "Irish Jew" is already to have told a joke, as almost any Irishman will be quick to inform you. And it's a joke that hasn't been mitigated, but only somehow enriched, by the election of a Jewish Lord Mayor of Dublin. But this is precisely the point, the point behind the point of *Ulysses*, isn't it? Jews and Irishmen alike feel this abiding—one is tempted to say eternal—archetypal conflict, this antipathy, this polar opposition, as essential in each case to their own identity, part of the very definition of themselves. It's hard to imagine a Jew who doesn't have hostile feelings about an Irishman, and Irishman who doesn't have resentful feelings about Jews. But both the Irish and the Jews feel this conflict (despite the history of real violence and persecution in Ireland and elsewhere) as *comic;* and in this sense, the relationship is unique. It's not true, for instance, of relations of Jews to Germans, or Jews to Poles, or Jews to Russians, with whom they are also in archetypal conflict. Only the archetypal conflict of the Jew and the Irishman is felt on both sides as essentially and radically comic, or at least somehow comic, comic after all.

Certainly (if I may be personal again and talk in terms of my own memory) it had, whatever it may have been in the Old Country, already become a joke in the America into which I was born, the New World to which both Jews and Irish had emigrated in large numbers, and where they both were beginning to achieve a spectacular kind of success. In the popular arts of my own childhood, at any rate, the conflict of the Irishman and the Jew had been turned into a laughing matter. I remember clearly, for instance, a famous comedy team called Gallagher and Sheen, whose patter songs were played on every Victrola, Irishman and Jew swapping gags, forerunners of George Burns and Gracie Allen, in whom the polar opposites, Jewish straight man and Irish zany had become man and wife. And everybody, I suppose, of a certain age in America remembers that longest running play of all time, that romantic comedy that possessed Broadway year after year, called *Abie's Irish Rose*, and in which, sentimentally and ridiculously, the old conflict was resolved.

But the comic conflict has been played out not only on records and radio and in literature, but in life as well; and in fact, it seems impossible, for a Jew at least, to escape it. Forgive me for speaking once more in terms of my own experience. In the course of my long trip to Ireland, to which I came in fact by way of Africa (being the kind of man who takes seriously the lesson learned from Joyce, that the longest way around is the shortest way home), I spent a week or so in Biafra, where that old joke, the joke of the conflict of the Jew and the Irishman was reenacted as if for my special benefit, to prepare me, perhaps, for this symposium. And I can't resist, therefore, telling you a story that makes the point I have been trying to establish with appropriately ridiculous clarity.

The scene is Biafra. I've come to find black Africa, and I discover that I am in the midst of the very white Holy Ghost Fathers in a mission where I have been given bed and board. I discover, in fact, that of the 200 white people in Biafra, 194 are Irish and the other 6 are Jewish, including me. As I sit at supper with the good Fathers, who have been telling me that I had better go to Dublin because I'd find there the shortest miniskirts in Europe, and would I please send them back some good Irish whiskey when I get there, suddenly one of them leans over—obviously knowing that I'm a Jew, just as I know that he's Irish, since we were intended to recognize each other from the beginning of time—and says "You people have always given us a lot of trouble."

For a moment or two, I thought he was talking about the Jew who, in fact, gave them the most trouble of all, namely Jesus, the son of Mary; but actually he was referring to the founder of his own order, who turns out to have been called Jacob Lieberman. Imagine that, you Joyceans, imagine how Joyce would have loved that. Jacob, the beloved man, beloved, darling Jacob, whose other name is Israel; but Seamus is jokey for Jacob, you remember Joyce told us, and Seamus is James, which is to say Joyce himself, Shem the Penman. At any rate, Jacob Lieberman founded the order of the Holy Ghost Fathers in 1858; "and," my friend the priest told me, "he sent all of us poor Irish out here to Africa, but like his kind, he remained behind in Paris."

Well, I recovered from Biafra, black and white, as one rises out of slow fever, as one wakes from the nightmare of history, and came to dear, dirty Dublin. And there I found myself at lunchtime the first day stuck between two colleagues at this symposium, each a proper anti-Semite after his kind: an Eastern European anti-Semite on my right hand, and an Irish anti-Semite on my left hand. And they began to engage in a conversation with each other, through me, over me, in which the subject being discussed really was which one of their peoples had the appropriate attitude toward the perfidious Jews.

The Eastern European anti-Semite started by boasting, "We're not unkind to the Jews, you understand. We let them go freely, leave, get out—whenever they want to. Why not?"

And when the question was asked what happens to them when they're uprooted from their homes, footloose and impoverished, he said, "Well, listen, what do they have to worry about—going out into a community that has millions stashed away in Swiss banks."

But this somehow did not satisfy the Irishman, who responded, "The real trouble is not with the Jews as Jews, it's with the Jews as Zionists. But after all, all Jews are Zionists because," I think I quote directly now, "none of them ever really becomes the citizen of anyplace." *None of them really ever becomes the citizen of anyplace.*

Once again we hear the voice of the Citizen in the Pub, and the biscuit box is ready to be hurled; once again we are back in *Ulysses*, that joke on all the Irish-Jewish jokes of history, which itself is no joke—though funny as any of them. And we remember that the reproach to the Jew is the artist's boast, that what is said of the Jew in contempt, Joyce said of himself in pride: "not a citizen of anyplace," which, if you'll pardon me for a final time, is the boast of the saint as well. Indeed, all three archetypal strangers, the Jew, the artist, and the saint, are never at home, never *quite* at home anywhere in this world, never quite the citizens of anyplace this side of Heaven.

But it's only the artist, a certain kind of artist, who makes his alienation a point of pride, thinks of it as separating him from rather than joining him to the rest of mankind. And this brings us back, by a commodious vicus of recirculation, to such insufferable prigs as poor Stephen, which is to say, to the part of Joyce that remained Stephen forever, try as he would. Yet it was not Joyce-Stephen who wrote *Ulysses*, it was Joyce-Bloom, the father begotten of the Son, the Jew born of the Irishman by the simple process of growing old.

In the middle of life, as the day wears on, we who began as

sons and lovers look around to discover that we have become fathers and husbands; that somehow we have learned exile is not what must be sought but what must be endured, and what therefore joins every man to every other man. This, at any rate, the part of Joyce that became Bloom learned well enough to write the book which he did not call, as he ought have, *A Portrait of Everyone as a No-Longer-Young Man;* but, instead, simply *Ulysses:* that absurd and moving account of a man no longer young, who, without illusion or self-deceit, goes home again, back to the ass that betrays him, the land that denies him, the son he does not and cannot ever really know. Moving from *A Portrait of the Artist* to *Ulysses,* we learn with Joyce that though it may be the self-pitying son who falls out of the air, it is the self-deprecating father who picks himself up off the hard earth again.

I would like to believe that even without the help of Joyce I might myself eventually have fought my way through to the place where I stand now, to a realization of what I now realize and have been saying to you. And maybe it must even be granted that I had to be where I am now before I could read properly his great and ambiguous novel, had myself to become Bloom before I could understand *Ulysses.* But certainly it is Joyce's mythological language that occurs to me talking about these matters, Joyce's mythological language in which I can best express what I am moved to tell not only you but myself as I approach my conclusion this evening.

Like many of you here before me, like Joyce himself, I began by thinking that I was Stephen; began by thinking I was the perpetual victim, perpetually stoned to death by his own infidel kin; began by thinking that I was the high-flying boy doomed to fall in glory and to write the story of my plunge earthward even as I fell. But I ended, as you will end, as Joyce ended, by knowing that I was Bloom, a comic, earthbound father who is also an Apostle to the Gentiles; which is to say, I have discovered at long last that I am a Hebrew of the Hebrews and a Pharisee of the Pharisees who, try as he will to be all things to all men, cannot resist, from time to time, still kicking against the pricks.

Joyce and Jewish Consciousness

WITH the French Revolution and the breakdown of the ghetto walls, which had for so long sealed them off from their gentile neighbors, Jews not merely entered the consciousness of Europe but began to find voices of their own, audible to gentile ears. From that point on, the *yiddisher kopf* has spoken to the *goyisher kopf*, the Jewish head to the gentile head, eventually changing the grid of perception through which both have perceived the world they share. Slowly a new Jewish mythology (created first by possessed gentiles, then by the Jews themselves) has penetrated the secular ideology of the West, quite as the older Jewish mythology of the Bible had long ago penetrated its theology. The Judeo-Christian God once dead (for the intellectuals of Europe, at least), Judeo-Christian science rushed in to fill the vacuum His demise had left. The name of the latter-day prophets of that science we all know: Marx, Freud, Einstein—vestigial, problematical, sometimes self-hating Jews; but somehow real Jews, all the same, in their heads if not their hearts or unbelieved-in souls. It was solely through the sciences, however, that the *yiddisher kopf* first spoke in gentile tongues: political economy, depth psychology, theoretical physics; and it is therefore apt that Joyce's Jew, Leopold Bloom, though a character in a novel, be a scientist manqué.

In literature, it took a longer time for actual Jewish voices to be heard and responded to. In English books, to be sure, there had been Jewish characters from the sixteenth century on, the Barabbas of Marlowe and Shakespeare's Shylock, for instance; and in the nineteenth century, they came thick and fast: Scott's Isaac of York, Dickens's Fagin, George Eliot's Daniel Deronda. But these remain ventriloquist's dummies: Jewish faces masking troubled gentile sensibilities or projecting gentile guilt and paranoia, not authentic Jewish heads prophesying a future inconceivable without them. Only when Jews became full citizens of the gentile Republic of Letters could true Jewish characters come to life, true Jewish myths begin to haunt the deep psyche of the Christian world. But long before Saul Bellow or Isaac Bashevis Singer had been granted the supreme gentile accolade of the Nobel Prize, Joyce had created in Bloom the first archetypal modern Jew: not ghettoized Israelite or Hebrew, but emancipated, secularized *yid*, his knowledge of his own ancestral tradition approaching degree zero without diminishing his Jewish identity.

Though certain eminent quasi- or half-Jewish modernists like Proust and Kafka were almost simultaneously dreaming their mythic *yids*, Swann and Joseph K., the latter do not have quite the authenticity or archetypal resonance of the character who takes over the last half of *Ulysses*, revealing Stephen Dedalus, who has first seemed the author's spokesman, as a bloodless, priggish and quite unmythological goy. But all of this seems fair enough in light of the fact that Joyce without a single drop of

"Jewish blood" had more of a "Jewish head" than either of his modernist contemporaries, or even the anti-Semitic Stephen, with whom he vainly sought to identify. Stephen is sketched from memory, a memento of a past his author had outgrown; but Bloom is drawn from life: based not on some Jew Joyce happened to have known, whether Italo Svevo or whomever, but on the self who was writing *Ulysses* at the same age that Leopold had reached in that fiction.

The invention of Bloom is, then, not so much an inspired act of impersonation as it is the Virgin birth of the sober Jew, who, Joyce reveals for the first time, lives within every drunken Irishman. It is an event matched only by Samuel Richardson's projection of the feminine in his own male psyche as Clarissa, the first great female character in the modern novel. Androgynous Bloom is, I am suggesting, as much an *anima* figure as Richardson's heroine, springing similarly full-grown from his author's splitting, hung-over head. But he has lived for a long time now (since 1934, in fact, when I first read *Ulysses*) in mine: that Jewish head conceived inside a Celtic one surviving inside the Jewish head I bear. It is not nearly as complicated as it sounds; or at least, it never seemed so to me until I heard Hugh Kenner assert from the very platform at St. Michael's College, University of Toronto, where I first made these remarks that a) Joyce is not really Celtic or Irish at all, but a sort of generalized European, while b) Bloom is not really a Jew either, but only a variant form of the same.

On the former question, I can speak with no real authority or passion. But on the latter, I can scarcely help talking with somewhat more assurance and considerably more feeling. I have long been aware that Hugh Kenner, like Ezra Pound, to whose modernist esthetics and anti-Semitic politics he responds with what I find queasy-making sympathy, is an archetypal *goyisher kopf*, as incapable of recognizing what is Irish as he is of acknowledging what is Jewish; for, mythologically speaking, they are the two complementary halves of a quite ungoyish unity. To my grandfather, from whom I first learned not just that I was a Jew, but what a Jew was, the term *goyisher kopf* meant merely a stupid head; it was what he called me whenever I proved inept or obtuse. But no one can (and I surely do not want to seem to) accuse Kenner of stupidity without seeming stupid himself. Yet his intelligence, however impressive, operates within heathen or pagan parameters, which disqualifies him, I think, from talking about certain aspects of Joyce, who was, whatever his quarrel with the Church of his mother, a Christian—which is to say, a Jew once removed, an inheritor of the promise made to our father Abraham by the Jewish God.

Kenner's trying to take Bloom away from the Jews is, consequently, both wrong and heretical in the light of the New Testament as well as the Old: a grosser heresy, in fact, than Sigmund Freud's attempt to prove that Moses was not a Jew, which denied only the latter. In response to Kenner, therefore, I am reclaiming Bloom for a second time (my earlier try, the essay called "Bloom on Joyce," I then thought of as my final word on the subject), by asserting yet again that no Jew has ever read *Ulysses* without recognizing Bloom as a fellow Jew, and rejoicing that this portrait of "one of Us" by "one of Them" (the last in a long series, which begins so dismally with Shylock and Fagin) is so sympathetic. Bloom is, finally, a gentile's Jew (the *only* gentile's Jew?) representing not some ultimate feared and hated other, but an essential aspect of the feared and beloved Self. Never mind that Joyce attributed to Bloom his own kinkiest sexual predilections; he turns out to be what can be adequately described only by another Yiddish word, a *mensch*; which is to say, a full male human being, as imagined by a tradition hostile to most of the qualities that the gentile world has thought of as being specifically macho.

If Joyce can be faulted at all for his treatment of Bloom, it is because he deals with him a little too sentimentally, responding as soft-heartedly as he does to dead mothers or children, to the plight of the persecuted Jew. It is as if he loses all objectivity and ironic detachment when dealing with the favorite butt of barroom bullies or cynical medical students, who—unlike Bloom or Stephen or Joyce himself—remain uncircumcised in the spirit, unchastened in their phallic pride; and are therefore contemptuous of all who have been. Many critics, including Hugh Kenner, fail to see, or are at any rate driven to deny, this "womanly" mawkishness in Joyce, preferring to dwell on his antisentimental irony; but he tends to betray it whenever he enters Bloom's Jewish heart and head. Joyce himself seems to have grown ashamed of this weakness in himself after Ulysses, eschewing it completely in the goyish pages of *Finnegans Wake*, where, for that reason among others, I prefer not to follow him.

In the Ithaca scene of *Ulysses*, however, to which Kenner did not allude at all in his contribution to the St. Michael's College symposium, but which is central to any real understanding of the dialogue between (vestigial) Jewish consciousness and (minimal) Celtic sensibility at the heart of Joyce's novel, the pathetic note persists beneath the ironical surfaces of the text. That penultimate episode is, to be sure, cast in the cool and very un-Jewish form of a catechism. Yet in it, for the first and last time in the book, an older Jew and a younger Irishman—spokesmen, respectively, for the middle-aged author who writes and the juvenile self he remembers—converse about their essential Jewishness and Irishness; and attempt to find, not so much in what each remembers, but in what each has forgotten, common ground. Behind this ironic, pathetic effort lies the desperate hope of establishing a father-son relationship of the spirit in place of the paternal-filial bond which has failed both in the flesh.

I can never reread this scene without thinking yet again of my own Jewish grandfather, since Stephen enters it still hopelessly drunk after a night out in a brothel presided over by a bad Jewish mother, a "madam." He embodies, that is to say, whoever has provided him the means to attain it, the condition that the first Yiddish song my grandfather taught me insists is the archetypal one of the gentile. "*Oi, oi, oi,*" that slanderous ditty runs, "*a shicker is a goy. Shicker is er, trinken mis er, veil er is a goy,*" meaning, "Oh, oh, oh, a drunkard is a gentile. A drunkard he is and drink he must, because he is a gentile." But Bloom, who guides and sustains Stephen on his way from the false Jewish house of Bella to his own real Jewish home, is, of course, stone-cold sober; for, according to the same song, "a Jew is sober and pray he must, because he is a Jew."

Leopold Bloom, however, who can make it all the way through no prayer in any language, settles for good deeds instead—more like a Samaritan than a Hebrew in this respect. He offers Stephen the secular refuge of his home, where he vainly tries to persuade him to tidy up. The notion of the "unwashed Bard" is one that offends his Jewish sensibility, as does Stephen's torn clothing, which he imagines having mended. Meanwhile, he prepares for him a nice cup of hot cocoa, behaving at this point more like a traditional Jewish mother than a mythological Jewish Father, though he never quite says, "Eat! Eat!"

Perhaps finally, though, it is as a nurturing Jewish Father that we must think of him, imagine him thinking of himself. And there is a model for this that has persisted in the collective unconscious of the gentile world, side by side with the more sinister figure of the Jewish Father with the knife, represented by Abraham, who begins by circumcising his son and ends by almost, almost taking away his life. That model is, of course, St. Joseph, impotent husband of the Blessed Virgin, foster-father of her (by him at least) unbegotten male child, patron saint of all cuckolds. Insofar as it is Bloom's book, though not in his sections alone, *Ulysses* is, like its author, haunted by threat of cuckoldry: cuckoldry as supreme dirty joke, as well as cuckoldry as inscrutable mystery. What child indeed knows his own father—for sure, for *sure?* In the novel, at any rate, the joke and the mystery become one: the sexual betrayal of Leopold by Molly in the arms of the supergoy, Blazes, is mythologically equated with that of Joseph by Mary—pregnant before he has ever bedded her, with a child sired, true believers say, by the Jewish God, but anti-Christian blasphemers insist by a wandering Roman soldier, not merely human but a goy. Malachi Mulligan, the novel's chief mocker, is forever playing with this ambiguous mystery-joke, singing the bawdy ballad of "Joseph the Joiner," alluding slyly to an anticlerical French version of the conversation between Mary and her impotent spouse, whose punch line runs: " '*Qui vous a mis dans cette fichue position?*' '*C'est le sacré pigeon, Joseph.*' " " 'Who got you into this frigging state?' 'It was the damned Dove, Joseph.' "

Joseph-Bloom, however, does not recount this imaginary dialogue, nor does he sing "Joseph the Joiner," being himself victim rather than mocker. He slanders no one in fact, certainly not Mary or the fruit of her womb, whom he thinks of as having been "a Jew like me." When he quotes scripture at all, it is likely to be the Old Testament or some garbled parody of the Talmud. So, for instance, in the Circe episode he chants a pseudolitany of pidgin Hebrew, which begins with the names of the first four letters of the Jewish alphabet, "Aleph Beth Ghimel Daleth" and ends with the oddly conjoined words, "Messhugah Talith," meaning "crazy prayer shawl." What he inadvertently travesties is not the language of Stephen's denied faith but of his own lapsed one. The alphabet of his ancestors especially haunts him, suggesting perhaps that if only he could remember it all, he could reconstruct his lost tradition; but three letters is the best he can do when he tries once more in the Ithaca section to draw for Stephen the characters in which God's word was first written. And after Stephen replies in kind by sketching the corresponding Celtic letters, he chants from the Song of Songs his approximation of the Hebrew for "thy temple amid thy hair is as a slice of pomegranate." But he knows no more than this of the mystic-erotic chant, of which the rabbis said that the day on which it was given to Israel was worth all the rest from the beginning of Creation; and he goes on to an even more mangled rendition of what he can recall of the Zionist anthem, *"Ha-tikvah,"* "The Hope."

Though the latter song was actually written in the nineteenth century, Stephen imagines it to be an archaic melody, stirring in him at any rate a sense of ancient and alien mysteries, which move him, oddly enough, to an anti-Semitic response. At any rate, he sings in return (wickedly? naively?) an old ballad called "The Jew's Daughter," which evokes, in a context of eros and castration fear, the ritual murder charges against the Jews that have haunted English poetry from the time of Chaucer on.

> She took a penknife out of her pocket
> And cut off his little head,
> And now he'll play his ball no more
> For he lies among the dead.

It does not seem to occur to Stephen that the Blessed Virgin is also a "Jew's Daughter." He thinks rather of the threat to gentile sexuality implicit in Judaism, recalling the myth of the castrating knife, held not by the bearded patriarch but by his surrogate, the smiling daughter. It is with little Harry Hughes, the martyred Christian boy, that Stephen identifies—as is, after all, appropriate enough to one whose given name is that of the first martyr to the Jews. And it is in self-pity that he recites the words: "Reluctant, unresistant, victim, predestined."

Ironically, however, Bloom is at the same time applying those terms to himself, a stranger in a strange land, whose head the jingoistic Citizen has tried to knock off just a little while before. Besides, he has a daughter of his own, whom he even imagines briefly holding Stephen in her arms. In his fantasy, however, her embrace (or alternatively, it occurs to him, his wife's, since the way to the daughter leads through the mother) is intended to lure Stephen over the wall that separates them not to death but to love, to life enriched, to Home. Why, then, does Stephen respond to this offer of Jewish hospitality, with all its erotic overtones, not just negatively, but with anti-Semitic slander? It is, in part, surely because an invitation to domesticity, Jewish or otherwise, seems to him the equivalent of castration, decapitation, death itself—the denial of his dream of an artist's freedom, more goyish than Jewish, more Hellenic than Hebraic. In any case, anti-Semitism is everywhere in *Ulysses* the chief, almost the sole mode of relating to Jews available to gentiles; and, indeed, it is only in response to it that Bloom can feel himself a Jew at all, since ritually and even ethnically he scarcely qualifies.

As Hugh Kenner has quite justly observed, Bloom, though twice baptized, has not been circumcised, nor has he gone through a Bar Mitzvah, which means that he has not been sealed as a Son of the Covenant either eight days after his birth, or on attaining his moral majority at age thirteen. Moreover, he does not have a Jewish mother; for the Orthodox, only Jewish matrilineal descent makes one a Jew. Yet neither Bloom himself nor any of the gentiles he encounters in his daylong odyssey through Dublin, doubts his Jewishness for a moment.

That identity is for him not optional, but given once and for all, whatever his own free choice, or indeed, that of his parents, might have been. He has *no* choice, being, in that terrible sense, "chosen," one of the "chosen people," his fate sealed into his flesh at the moment of begetting, like some unerasable stigma. Even as he cannot unwill his destiny, he cannot flee it. Stephen can choose exile as a way of escaping the tradition into which he was born; but for the Jew, exile is, has been since the Diaspora, the expulsion from the Holy Land, the very essence of his mythic-ethnic condition. Zionism, at the fictional moment of *Ulysses,* or for that matter, even the moment of its actual writing, was not a political reality but a dream memorialized in the song Bloom, like many secular Jews, cannot quite remember. Even for himself, at that point the Jew is still the "Wandering Jew" of Christian legend, eternally not at home, as those who are, in whatever place he finds himself, constantly remind him.

We know finally that Bloom is a Jew, even as he himself knows it, because to him alone this is no joke. He cannot even laugh when the standard anti-Semitic quips are made, being himself their occasion and their butt, but winces or cries out in self-defense, "Christ was a Jew like me," stirring in his auditors only more sniggering. But Joyce does not snigger. To him the fact that Christ was a Jew seems no more a joke than that Odysseus was a Jew—not just in his travesty-epic, but, he firmly believes, from the very start, an archetypal Semite imagined by a Semitic bard. To compound the irony, Joyce further suggests that the Semitic bard was a woman. But the gender ambiguity is perhaps already implicit in the ethnic one, since Bloom has been portrayed as being, like all Jews, perhaps, more like what the gentiles mean by a "woman" than what they call a "man": androgynous at least, and in the moment of magical transformation in Circe's palace, when each is revealed visibly as what he has been invisibly all along, totally female. Metaphorically, mythologically, the novel suggests, "Jew" equals "woman" (as is symbolically indicated by circumcision) equals "blind poet": signifying *all* blind poets, we are left free to surmise, including not only Homer, but the myopic Irishman retelling the tale of Ulysses in exile from his homeland.

In Trieste, indeed, where Joyce finished his modern Irish version of the ancient Semitic epic, writing in the stranger language of the Sassenachs (his own ancestral tongue long forgotten), and going off to teach in an even more alien language, his predicament was more like that of Bloom in a country of Christian Celts than that of Stephen, who, however alienated, moved among his own blood kind in a land where for countless generations his ancestors had been born. There were, in fact, more Jews than Irish in the multiethnic enclave on the Adriatic, and apparently Joyce found many of his closest friends (plus one true love) among them. Often, therefore, he must have felt himself (his name, after all, being James or Seamus, which is to say Jacob or Israel) not the Jews' martyr like Stephen, but the Jews' Jew: an ultimate exile in an unredeemably foreign city, where he first imagined, then became, Bloom: a *yiddisher kopf* lost in the nightmare of goyish history, from which, as he wrote, we all strive vainly to awake.

The Christian-ness of the
Jewish-American Writer

MANY critics have for many years now been re-
marking (some in anger and sorrow, some—including me—
with detached amusement) the paradoxical fact that the rise of
Jewish-American literature to a dominant position in the culture
of the modern world occurred at a moment when the Jewishness
of the Jewish-American community had become problematical,
and indeed its very existence was being threatened by intermarriage, assimilation, and cultural attrition. It is a common-
place to observe that, in any case, most of the American writers
of Jewish ancestry, who from the late forties to the early sixties
were the most highly visible and most influential of our authors
and are still adulated and emulated wherever our books are read
(and where are they not?), were only vestigially, marginally,
minimally Jewish in any traditional sense of the word. By and
large the children of parents already in flight from the ghetto
and all it entails, they (or rather let me say "we," since I consider

myself one of them) were, in this sense at least, heirs of the Enlightenment, which had made that flight possible.

To be sure, some of us—in the aftermath of Hitlerism—sought to rediscover our roots, sentimentalizing the shtetl in retrospect; and, typically, reading Martin Buber to learn about Hasidism or Gershom Scholem to discover who Sabbatai Zevi really was. We tended, that is to say, to return to our religious heritage at secondhand, few of us acquiring even a nodding acquaintance with Rashi or Maimonides. Whatever Jewishness, therefore, we eventually stuffed into our already overstuffed heads, in our deep psyches almost no traces of traditional Jewish mythology and theology survived. But the deep psyche, like nature itself, abhors a vacuum and into its vacant spaces rushed images and archetypes, which we had acquired at firsthand during our acculturation in a Christian society.

But here precisely in the situation of the Jewish-American writer is a second paradox, which I have been able to realize only now that our rise to dominance has become a matter of history, and young Americans, with artistic ambitions, whether Jewish or gentile, no longer respond passionately to, much less seek to emulate, writers like Saul Bellow, whose Nobel Prize seems, as it were, posthumous, a belated tribute to a vanishing and irrecoverable past. Certainly, I myself have not until quite recently ever said publicly, or quite confessed even to myself, that when the Jewish-American writers of my own generation have—usually despite themselves or only half-aware—moved into the traditional provinces of religion and mysticism, from which the Enlightenment presumably delivered them, it was to Christian mythology and theology that they turned in quest of images and themes. Appropriately enough it was in Israel, at Bar-Ilan University, a bastion of Orthodoxy (mine was the only bare male head in what seemed more a congregation than an audience), that I began these meditations with some remarks on the Jewish-American writer and the legend of the Holy Grail.

That legend was just then much on my mind, since at that very moment a movie was being shot in the city in which I live, based (only approximately it turned out, of course) on Bernard Malamud's *The Natural*, a novel for which I felt a special affection, as I had, in the early fifties, helped rescue it from the undeserved oblivion to which it had been consigned by its earliest reviewers. My own review was, it seems to me now looking back, more impassioned panegyric than real analysis; though I did point out the hitherto unnoticed fact that beneath Malamud's story of an ill-fated baseball team, reminiscent of "those bums," the old Brooklyn Dodgers, lies an encrypted, ironic version of the Grail legend. Moreover, as I also tried to make clear, that version is based not on such traditional sources as Malory's *Morte d'Arthur* or Chrétien de Troyes's *Perceval* but on T. S. Eliot's retelling of that many-times-retold tale at a moment when he was seeking an escape from madness by returning to a still-not-quite-believed-in Christianity.

Why the other early commentators on *The Natural* had not perceived this, I still find inexplicable. After all, Malamud, like a good graduate student, makes painfully clear his debt to Eliot as well as the parallels of his tale to the Grail legend. He calls his clearly allegorical ballclub, for instance, the Knights, and its manager Pop Fisher: an allusion, clear to fellow graduate students, at least, to the Fisher King who presides over the Grail Castle in the original myth and is reevoked in *The Waste Land* in the lines "While I was fishing in the dull canal . . . / Musing upon the King my brother's wreck . . ."

In retrospect, however, I find little pride in having pointed out so obvious a fact, since I failed to perceive its only slightly less obvious implications: the final significance of a writer who, his earlier short stories having won him the reputation of being "the most Jewish of modern Jewish-American writers," in his first novel reimagines with an all-gentile cast (it is appropriate that thirty years later his hero be played by that prototypical *shegetz*, Robert Redford) a myth Christian in its final form though pagan in its roots, but in any case essentially goyish.

Before I could come to terms with this, I had first to come to a deeper understanding of that myth; by realizing that its central figure, the knight who achieves the Grail quest, whether called Perceval or Galahad, is Jewish: the direct descendant of Joseph of Arimathea, the shadowy Jewish patriarch who smuggled the cup from which Jesus drank at the Last Supper to a hiding place in England. The Jewishness of the Grail knight is hardly a secret, though it is a fact that seems to have given small comfort to either Jews or gentiles—as I was recently reminded in the course of reading *Deadeye Dick* by Kurt Vonnegut, Jr. in which a minor character asks rather plaintively why Jews who are always claiming Jesus as one of their own do not boast that Sir Galahad was one, too.

But the situation is more complex than Vonnegut suggests: as I explain in the essay (elsewhere in this book) called "Why Is the Grail Knight Jewish?" Galahad is a last, a terminal Jew, whose descendants (eternally virgin, he begets no fleshly offspring) are spiritual rather than physical children of Israel. Indeed, his legend, like an alternative myth to the Gospel story itself, symbolizes the transfer of God's promise from the East to the West, from the Jews to the gentiles. Like the Gospel story, too, the Grail legend is essentially anti-Semitic—the earliest written text in which it survives, Chrétien de Troyes's *Perceval*, ends with a vituperative outburst directed against the unconverted children of Abraham, "the wicked Jews, whom one should kill like dogs . . ."

Nor is it only in his somewhat uncharacteristic first novel that

Malamud evokes the Grail legend; he returns to it again and again (there have been Ph.D. dissertations written to demonstrate this) even in those of his fictions whose protagonists are Jews rather than goyim.

Moreover, he is by no means the only distinguished Jewish-American writer of his generation whose imagination was triggered by the myth of a quest for a sacred vessel whose discovery will bring back fertility to a parched land. As its title makes quite clear, so also was Saul Bellow in *Henderson the Rain King*, which, aptly enough, was until recently the only of his novels without a major Jewish character. To be sure, the explicit ideology of Bellow's comic fantasy is derived not from Christian sources but from the cult beliefs of black Africa as interpreted by certain Western anthropologists, most of them Jewish; though occasionally his putative sub-Saharan shamans spout ideas directly quoted from the post-Freudian psychology of Wilhelm Reich. It is, however, hard to believe finally that Bellow was not also influenced by T. S. Eliot, remote as his neo-orthodoxy is from such pagan gurus. Certainly, Henderson himself rather improbably quotes from that poet on occasion; and Bellow knew Eliot well enough, apparently, to collaborate in Isaac Rosenfeld's parodic translation of "The Love Song of J. Alfred Prufrock" into Yiddish.

There is, in any case, a special affinity—however ambivalent, puzzling, and perverse—between this expatriate High Church anti-Semite, for whom the entry of the Jews into gentile culture was a nightmare ("The rats are underneath the piles./The jew is underneath the lot"), and certain self-declared freethinking Jews who for a little while threatened to replace WASPs like him as spokesmen for their country and its culture. These included, along with Malamud and Bellow, certain of their most distinguished forerunners in the thirties, most notably, perhaps, Henry Roth, that writer whose rediscovery after World War II (in which I am proud of having played a part) marked the beginning of the emergence of Jewish-American literature to full visibility.

From the start, Roth's rediscoverers were aware of the pervasive influence of James Joyce on *Call It Sleep*. Indeed, it is apparent everywhere in the structure and texture of that novel—especially in its adaptation of "stream of consciousness." But few of us at first (certainly not I) perceived Roth's indebtedness to T. S. Eliot, which Roth himself, however, has since insisted was primary. Reminiscing in 1979, for instance, on the reading that inspired him to create his single novel, he told an interviewer, "and finally I came on *The Waste Land* . . . I must have read that *Waste Land* until I memorized it. Eliot became a tremendous influence on me . . ." Then he added, rather defensively, "I realized that there was this anti-Semitism, but I was willing to accept it. I thought, 'He isn't saying too much I haven't already observed among the Jews and disliked . . .' " Then he continued, switching defensively into the second person, "You thought it referred to the side of Judaism you had come to dislike in the first-generation Jews who had to subordinate everything in order to make some kind of economic base for themselves . . ."; after which he concluded, "So I would say that Eliot was the major influence on my life."

I must confess that I found this declaration of indebtedness a little astonishing; though I never doubted for a moment that *Call It Sleep* was, like *The Waste Land,* not merely a work with a religious subject but a religious work—despite its author's theoretical commitment to Marxist materialism, the account of a mystical revelation. But it had seemed to me originally an essentially Judaic book, at the farthest possible remove from Christian mythology and theology. After all, I told myself, it is our own Isaiah whose words echo and re-echo through the head of David Shearl, Roth's troubled young protagonist. I have, however, come slowly to realize that the *Haftorah* passage from the prophet of priestly caste, which so obsesses David, includes not just the image of the burning coal held to that prophet's unclean lips, but the verses, "For a child is born to us / A son is given unto us / And the government is on his shoulders." But this has, of course, been read by Christian interpreters as a prophecy of the coming of Christ, the Son of God, the Son of Man, the Suffering Servant (also a metaphor kidnapped out of Isaiah by Christologists), the Redeemer of Fallen Humanity. That Roth thought of humanity as fallen no reader of *Call It Sleep* has ever doubted; and Roth himself has declared, "there is one theme I like above all others, and that is redemption." Clearly, in the fable of redemption which is *Call It Sleep*, David plays the role of the redeemer—reenacting, this time around, not the Grail quest but an *imitatio Christi*.

Nor is Roth alone among the major Jewish-American writers of our country in this paradoxical and perverse—but also ironically apt—identification of the American son of a Jewish mother harried out of Eastern Europe by believing Christians with the Son of God in whose name they harried her. I recall, for instance, a climactic scene from Arthur Miller's *After the Fall* (its very title a giveaway), in which the crypto-Jewish protagonist stands front-stage center, his arms stretched out, his head bowed on his breast: the very image of the crucified Savior of the gentiles. And I remember, too, J. D. Salinger's insufferable Seymour Glass, whose death by his own hand—presumably for all of our sins—is memorialized in a pair of stories called *Franny and Zooey*, one of which centers on a prayer consisting of the single phrase, "Lord Jesus Christ, have mercy on me"; while the other ends with the revelation that "the Fat Lady," avatar of the Popular Audience, is also the avatar of the living God-Man of the Christians: "Ah buddy. Ah buddy. It's Christ Himself. Christ Himself, buddy."

An even more egregious example of Jewish Christolatry is to be found in the four short novels of the thirties writer who was by all odds the favorite literary ancestor of my own generation, however he may have been ignored in his own time. Born Nathan Wallenstein Weinstein, he sought to conceal his ethnic identity by renaming himself Nathanael West; but he made no attempt to hide his own mythological identification and that of his characters with the self-proclaimed Jewish messiah rejected by his own people. Three of his fictions, *Miss Lonelyhearts, A Cool Million,* and *The Day of the Locust,* end with the sacrificial deaths of their protagonists—none of whom, to be sure, are portrayed as Jews. In the first of these, the major character, an advice-to-the-lovelorn columnist, aspires to the role of the Crucified Christ, whom he thinks of as "The Miss Lonelyhearts of Miss Lonelyhearts." We first see him, indeed, alone in a cell-like chamber whose sole decoration is a crucifix nailed to the wall with large iron spikes; and when we see him last he is reaching out in Christlike, all-forgiving love to his worst enemy. To be sure, that enemy is not converted by his love but shoots him dead, which serves, of course (despite the irony with which the scene is rendered) to reinforce rather than undercut his identification with the mythological Son of Man.

Miller and Salinger and West, however, sought to conceal or camouflage, or at the very least to distance themselves from, their Jewishness, so that it is finally neither astonishing nor disturbing that they evoke in the place of Jewish myths the reigning archetypes of the gentile culture to which their very books represent an attempt at assimilating. But Henry Roth is another matter, being in most ways the farthest thing imaginable from a crypto-Jew. Many years ago in fact, I referred to *Call It Sleep* as "a specifically Jewish book, the best single book both by a Jew and about Jewishness written in America"; and in a sense I still believe this to be true. Certainly, whatever his debt to Joyce and Eliot, the words that ring in the ears of his protagonist at home and in the *heder* are Yiddish, Hebrew, and Aramaic; and the language he speaks on the street is the not-quite-English of the ghetto, in which the name of the Christian savior survives only as a cussword.

Where, then, I am left wondering, did Roth, whose linguistic and cultural world was identical with his fictional David's, learn to think of Christ as a model and prototype for his surrogate, the small, irredeemably Jewish boy seeking to redeem the filthy world into which he had been born? Not in the churches of the gentiles or in their scriptures, but (as we have already noticed) in the literature of High Modernism, particularly the poetry of T. S. Eliot. But how did he encounter Eliot in the first place? It is a question the answer to which will cast light not only on Roth's special case, but will provide a clue to the source of the Christian-ness of all Jewish-American writers—including me. It is, therefore, in reflecting on that answer, and all it implies, that I pose to conclude these meditations. And to find it one need look no further than the dedication of *Call It Sleep*, which reads: "To Eda Lou Walton."

It is a name once well-known in academic circles, though remembered now, if at all, only by those interested in Henry Roth: the name of a critic of modernist literature and professor of English at New York University whom Roth met while he himself was still a student at City College. Walton eventually became a kind of mistress-mother to this considerably younger Jew-boy from the ghetto, nurturing him through the grimmest years of the Great Depression. Not only did she enable him to write in economic security the one novel he ever managed to finish (meanwhile creating in him, perhaps, the guilt that may explain in part his succeeding long silence); she continued also, for as long as their relationship lasted, to act as his mentor. It was she who simultaneously inducted him into the mysteries of

The Communist Manifesto and introduced him to the work of the pioneers of High Modernism, especially Joyce and Eliot. Neither of them seems to have been troubled by the contradiction between the art-religion implicit in the latter and the secular faith of a world without God implicit in the former. Nor was she apparently much disturbed by the fact that most of the High Modernists she taught him to love were not merely anti-Semites but reactionaries, more often than not downright fascists.

In any case, both Marxism and modernism seemed to Roth to provide ways of revolting against the values of his parents, their vestigial Orthodox Judaism and their aspiration to make it at whatever cost in the crass bourgeois world; and also against the equally bourgeois (though considerably more genteel) late Victorian values which still influenced the teaching of literature when he was an undergraduate. Besides, it was (was it not?) the technique rather than the politics of modernists that he sought to emulate. But inevitably his work was also influenced by the myths that informed their experiments in symbolism and stream of consciousness, myths rooted in a religious tradition not merely non-Jewish but anti-Jewish. Like Roth, moreover, many more recent Jewish-American writers (including Malamud and Bellow and me) were similarly the victims/beneficiaries of goyish school mistresses and masters with avant-garde pretensions, who (even when they did not bed us down) tried with a passion no less intense for being totally sublimated, to induct us into the chic politics and esthetics of the modernist era.

That process of cultural assimilation began for us long before we reached the university—as early, indeed, as the compulsory first twelve years of our education, in which typically our classrooms were presided over by gentiles. I myself, for instance, in grade school had no Jewish teachers and in high school only one—married, as it happened, to a shikse and declared officially dead by his Orthodox family. Even as they taught me to pass by learning to speak the brand of standard English spoken in the gentile suburbs, they sought to impose on me a life-style utterly alien to that of my ancestors. The brainwashing process began with my first exposure to those insufferably pink-and-white role models, Dick and Jane, and ended with literature classes aimed at persuading me that I was the cultural heir of Longfellow, Whittier, and Holmes, Shakespeare and Milton, Wordsworth and Dickens. Nor did it help very much when I began to read behind the backs of those teachers more recent and still forbidden authors like Ezra Pound and D. H. Lawrence, Ernest Hemingway and Scott Fitzgerald.

Whatever I read in school or out, the pattern of my education was determined by the calendar of the Christian year, with school breaks and appropriate drawings on the blackboard at Christmas and Easter: all serving to remind me of my exclusion as a Jew from the shared joy of my gentile classmates. How I longed for a Christmas tree at home, even as I longed for a father who would play ball with me on a well-tended lawn like the "funny, funny father" of Dick and Jane. In addition, we still had in those bad old days compulsory school prayers; we all rose and bowed our heads for the recitation of the Lord's Prayer, which I refused to say of course, mumbling obscenities to myself instead, since it was *their* Lord we addressed, not mine.

But whatever I did I could not cancel out the fact that my first acquaintance—like that of my Jewish contemporaries who were to produce the most admired books of the post–World War II era—even with the portion of the Bible to which I permitted myself to listen, the specifically Jewish books, which I had been taught to call, Christian-style, "The Old Testament," I listened to in the King James version. Consequently, when in later years I tried to recapture the biblical tradition of my own people, it was in Christian terms that I reimagined it;

speaking, for instance, of "the Sacrifice of Isaac" rather than "the Binding," the *Akedah*. Indeed, to this very day I find it well-nigh impossible to picture the bound, but of course never sacrificed (that is the whole point of the tale), son of Abraham as the thirty-year-old man the rabbis insist he was rather than the helpless child portrayed in the galleries and described in the literature of the gentile world. Certainly, he appears so in my dreams, whatever my conscious mind tells me; and it is from such dreams that the books I and my Jewish-American contemporaries have since created are born.

Nor is this the final indignity: not only do the Jewish-American writers I have been discussing tend to read Jewish scripture through Christian eyes, but their perception of their own Jewishness is similarly secondhand; and they are consequently forever incapable of escaping the nightmare myths of themselves as the rejecters of the Messiah, the Killers of Christ. It is an accusation not only shouted at them or whispered behind their backs by yahoos, but one confirmed and reinforced by many of the Great Books their loving teachers taught them to perceive as their own, and which they themselves have come to love and emulate: for instance, Shakespeare's *The Merchant of Venice*, Dickens's *Oliver Twist*, and Chaucer's "The Prioress's Tale." However much they may have admired such classic writers, though, young American Jews, who in the thirties and earliest forties dreamed of some day writing books that would be read side by side with them and assigned like them in classes in English (and, improbably enough, succeeded), did not identify with them, anymore than they did with the Jewish grandparents they had never really known. They therefore had little trouble in dismissing the anti-Semitism in such books as the prejudices of another time and place. But what were they to do when they discovered similar anti-Semitic myths at the heart of modernist masterpieces by Eliot and Pound, whom they loved as older siblings, creators of an artistic mode of which they were (they dearly hoped) the heirs apparent.

Taking possession of that heritage, they assimilated, adapted, introjected myths deeply rooted in a religion utterly alien and indeed hostile to that of their own forebears. Not that any of them became, whatever twinges of self-hatred they endured, overt or conscious anti-Semites. But they did, below the level of full consciousness, identify their most sympathetic characters, the surrogates for their essential selves, with archetypal terminal "good Jews" (good precisely because they were terminal), like the Grail knight and the Crucified Christ. And so also they identified those who rejected their own experimental art, the despised philistines—including their own kin, who had shamelessly made it in bourgeois America—with the "bad Jews" condemned in the New Testament and excoriated in the diatribe that climaxes Chrétien de Troyes's *Perceval.*

But this troubling paradox is further complicated by the fact (of which I have only recently become aware—finding in that awareness a kind of wry consolation) that the same situation has prevailed ever since Christianity began to define itself against Judaism. From the very start, that is to say, the archetypal heroes of gentile literature, whether sacred or secular, from Jesus to Galahad and Perceval, have been portrayed as birthright Jews. Moreover, the earliest texts in which they appeared were written by birthright Jews, from Matthew and Mark to Chrétien de Troyes: vestigial Jews, to be sure, like Bellow, Malamud, Roth, West, and Salinger, who—paradoxically, ironically—Judaized the Christian culture to which they assimilated, even as they Christianized the Jewish tradition out of which they came.

Isaac Bashevis Singer; or
The American-ness of the
American-Jewish Writer

In his Nobel Prize acceptance speech, Isaac Bashevis Singer made it clear that he considered the award a tribute not to him but to the language in which he writes, a language without a homeland and—in the opinion even of most living Jews—without a future. There seems little doubt, moreover, that the Committee which bestowed that award must have agreed with him, since they could not otherwise have honored him so soon after Saul Bellow, another Jew who lives and writes in the United States. To that Committee, I must suppose, Bellow seemed an *American* novelist, and Singer a *Jewish* one; but the matter is by no means clear-cut. To the Jewish literary establishment, for instance, the majority of critics who read him in Yiddish, Singer's work seems too demonic and erotic to be properly "Jewish" at all; and they are, therefore, profoundly uneasy that he has been taken by the gentile world as representing a culture they feel he traduces and betrays.

It was not the Yiddishists but precisely such Jewish-American writers as Bellow (who began the whole process by translating "Gimpel the Fool"), Isaac Rosenfeld, and Irving Howe who introduced Singer first to a larger American public without Yiddish, then to the world. Singer has always insisted on his difference from such Jewish-American exponents of "modern" fiction, alienated from their folk roots and too highfalutin to tell a simple story; so that there seems no reason to disbelieve him when he says he has never read any of them. But they have read and loved him for the very reasons surely that his fellow fictionists in Yiddish have rejected him, finding in his obsession with sex and his evocation of demons an assurance that he is "one of them."

Much time has elapsed, however, between the publication of those earliest translations and the Nobel Prize; and our culture has changed so much that these days one is more likely to find a new Singer story Englished in the *New Yorker* than in journals like *Partisan Review, Commentary,* or *Midstream,* in which he made his American debut. He has passed, that is to say, from the pages of magazines devoted to building a bridge between secular Jewish culture or, more generally, secular European culture, and American culture, to those of one which aspires to be the epitome of *goyish* America; and seems more suitable, therefore, to the fiction of John Cheever, John Updike, and Donald Barthelme than to fantasies dreamed in exile by a child of the Warsaw ghetto.

Despite the fact that he continues to write in Yiddish for *The Daily Forward* topical essays, reminiscences, uncollected tales, serial installments of novels, all under the name of "Isaac Warshafsky," Singer has created for himself—after forty-five years in the United States— another, an American persona called "Isaac Bashevis Singer." Under that name, he now publishes in English *for the first time* all his books, whether novels or collections of short fiction. Even when he still permitted full-length volumes of his work to make their initial appearance in Yiddish, he did so under a third name, "Isaac Bashevis," a matronymic he bestowed on himself in honor of his mother, Bathsheba. Son of his native city as a journalist, son of his mother as a Yiddish novelist, he is his father's son as an American author; or perhaps rather the acknowledged brother of Israel Joshua Singer, that beloved and resented sibling rival, who became an American author before him—creating for Isaac a writer's block he could not break from the moment of his arrival on this soil until the latter's premature death.

Though he still does the first version of almost everything he writes in Yiddish, what he chooses to preserve between hard covers the twiceborn Singer now turns before final publication (with the help of translators and editors, though, one gathers, more and more subject to his own final judgment) into English, American English, American. This seems fair enough, inevitable perhaps, in light of the fact that that language has become for the majority of surviving Jews the *mammeloshen,* a secular mother tongue, filling the function once served by Aramaic, Ladino, and Yiddish itself. But what this means in Singer's case is that his fiction is not merely read, received, and reviewed in American English, but exported to Europe, East and West, and to the Third World along with other items of Jewish-American culture, including the novels of Saul Bellow, Bernard Malamud, and Philip Roth. It was, therefore, as an American as well as a Jew that most of the world perceived Singer at the moment of his receiving the Nobel Prize—whatever he or the Committee believed, or pretended to believe.

But he is, of course, though an American and a Jew and a writer, *not* a Jewish-American writer like Bellow or Malamud or Roth. He is rather an American-Jewish writer: the only truly distinguished fictionist, perhaps (his brother Israel Joshua and

Sholem Asch once seemed contenders, but they fade fast from our memories), to have arisen from among ex-European Jews entering the United States after the closing down of mass immigration. In his own awareness and in ours, he has never seemed an "immigrant" as defined by earlier, first-generation Jews from the Pale, like Anzia Yezierska or Abraham Kahan. Nor is he perceived as a "refugee." These came later, out of the heart of the Holocaust, which Singer is constantly aware of having missed, thus remaining unredeemably a survivor of but not a participant in the destruction of Eastern European Jewry. In this sense, he is more like us second- and third-generation offspring of earlier immigrants, than the escapees from Nazi concentration camps or Stalin's Siberia who, to be sure, populate his fiction.

Like them, however, and unlike us, his first tongue is Yiddish and his earliest memories belong to the shtetl and the Warsaw ghetto. He is, in short, an *emigré* (something for which there is no exact word in our language): one whose identity is involved with a dead past rather than an unborn future; one who seeks not to lose but forever to cling to his status as an unreconstructed greenhorn, unassimilated, incapable of assimilation to American culture. He remains eternally—in theory, at least—a member of no community except that essentially stateless one which remembers not only Yiddish and *Yiddishkeit*, but the alliances and rivalries, the parochial politics, the hates and loves of a Yiddish-speaking intelligentsia, made up of men and women, long dead, or reduced to silence, or scattered over the face of the earth. The aging survivors of that community, though rescued from terror and living in relative security, tend to think of themselves condemned to perpetual exile, whether they find themselves in Montreal or Buenos Aires or Tel Aviv or New York, or even a Kiev or an Odessa or a Warsaw transformed beyond recognition.

The protagonists of Singer's stories with a contemporary setting find themselves from time to time in one or another of those places of exile, chiefly, of course, New York, the city in which he has lived for some four decades and a half. He has, to be sure, moved back and forth across our land during that time, spending occasional semesters in residence at Oberlin and the University of Wisconsin, and making overnight lecture stops everywhere in the cornfields and wheatfields of the heart of the heart of this country. By and large, however, he portrays America—his second homeland—as a claustrophobic enclave, centered in the West Side of Manhattan, and bordered on one side by Coney Island, on the other by the resort towns of the Catskill mountains. Nonetheless, more and more of his fiction takes place in that narrow American world, including three novels, *Enemies, A Love Story; Shadows by the Hudson;* and *A Ship to America* (the latter two, ironically enough, never translated from their serialized Yiddish versions in *The Daily Forward*) and some twenty-five short stories. I have read most though not all of the shorter fiction, and, of course, only the novel in English; but that has been enough to pose for me— urgently, tantalizingly—the question of what exactly is American about Singer's American fiction?

Perhaps because I have spent many years speculating on the Jewishness of the Jewish-American writer, and have vowed I will return to it no more, I turn with a real sense of relief to the complementary one: What *is* the American-ness of the American-Jewish writer? Minimal, I am tempted to say, thinking of Singer, almost nonexistent: an American-ness degree zero, equal and opposite to the Jewishness degree zero of such vestigially Jewish-American novelists as Nathanael West, J. D. Salinger, Bruce Jay Friedman, or, for that matter, myself. The characters in Singer's American stories and his American novel move through a putatively American landscape consisting of mean city streets, where the temperature is always too hot or too cold, and the gray rain ceases only to let the gray snow fall.

There are other American novels set in similar urban landscapes; but in Melville's *Pierre* or even Saul Bellow's *The Victim*, somehow we are aware that somewhere beyond the asphalt and concrete there is a Wilderness, unlimited space, the untamed ocean. But outside of Singer's half mythological city, we are permitted to imagine only squalid bungalows huddled on the slopes of alien hills; and if the sea laps the shores of his Coney Island, it remains always a sea seen from apartment house windows, into whose waves his protagonists are never moved to plunge. Those protagonists tend to fade into each other in the American tales, seeming at last variations of a single antihero who uncannily resemble his author.

Whatever alternative lives Singer creates for him, he sees always in his mirror the same face, white-skinned, blue-eyed, red-headed but balding fast. Moreover, he is inevitably a crusading vegetarian, a nonsmoker, a moderate man without a passion for drink (in a land where whiskey is more myth than intoxicant, more Muse than myth); a Yiddish journalist and traveling lecturer; a reader of occultist magazines, forever questing for a God in whose goodness he finds it even harder to believe than in his existence. Endlessly, restlessly, though self-tormentingly polygamous, he is sometimes married and sometimes not, but always essentially a bachelor; and he yearns, even more than he does for God, for an equally polygamous female: a witch, a *revenant*, or a woman possessed, with whom he can achieve a kind of living *Liebestod*, a kind of *eros* indistinguishable from *thanatos*.

That protagonist—though his alter ego, the author, exists for his audiences only in English—lives in his dreams and waking fantasies only in Yiddish, and consequently, meets only speakers of Yiddish, *emigrés* like himself, in his wanderings through a psychedelic landscape, whose street signs and billboards are written in English, yet which remain in many ways disconcertingly non-American. Not only does he encounter no Red Men in the streets he walks (how could he, after all?), but though the city he haunts (or is haunted by) is recognizably New York, even blacks remain always on the periphery, intangible, almost invisible: half-naked savages on the edge of vision—a troublemaker in the subway, a bootblack tickling his toes as he slops polish on his shoes. Indeed, there are scarcely any white American goyim in his fictions, not as expected persecutors, not as improbable lovers. Never a *shegetz*. And when a shikse enters the scene, she is likely to be a European, a peasant, a servant girl from the shtetl.

Small wonder, then, that the myth of interethnic male bonding, present in all authentic American fiction from James Fenimore Cooper to Mark Twain and Ken Kesey (even turning up in Bellow's *Henderson the Rain King* and Malamud's *The Tenants*) is absent from his pages. There is, in fact, almost *no* male bonding in Singer's overwhelmingly heterosexual world. What we find instead is domestic strife and joy, demonic love; and, especially, a desperate metaphysical joining of male and female flesh, which goes beyond the erotic mysticism of the *Zohar* into the realm of heresy: a triumphant celebration of what is perverse and forbidden in passion—incestuous, adulterous, necrophiliac, Satanic love in the mode of Sabbatai Zevi.

And yet—and *yet*, very occasionally, through the eyes of one or another of his tormented, vegetarian nympholepts, Singer sees in America suggestions for new heresies, more appropriate to the end of the twentieth than the close of the seventeenth century, and discoverable perhaps only in a world in which he can never feel really at home. One notable instance occurs near the conclusion of an American story called "The Third One." The theme, an "unnatural triangle" involving the bonding of husband, wife, and lover, comes right out of Dostoyevsky; but its climactic moment of vision occurs in Times Square as his first-person narrator, sweltering in the subtropical heat of midsummer Manhattan, looks up at the electric billboard display:

"We walked out on Broadway," he tells us, "and the heat hit me like a furnace. It was still daylight but the neon signs were already lit, announcing in fiery language the bliss to be brought by Pepsi-Cola, Bond suits, Camel cigarettes, Wrigley's chewing gum. A tepid stench came up from the subway gratings." Though this begins like an infernal scene, it is presided over by no familiar European devil; only the image (portrayed on a movie house billboard) of "a half-naked woman four stories high, lit up by spotlights—her hair disheveled, her eyes wild, her legs spread out, a gun in each hand. Around her waist was a fringed scarf that covered her private parts." And when Zelig Fingerbein, who has just told the tale of his wife and live-in lover, stops to stare, "one eye laughing and one tearing," the narrator beside him is moved to say, "If there is no God, she is our god." To which Zelig, shaking "as if he had been awakened from a trance," responds, " 'What *she* is promising she can deliver.' "

Though they can comment on, gloss the American scene, such choral voices cannot be understood by American passersby. The language they speak is dying or dead, though they do not know it, being themselves a kind of living dead—either living European Jews who do not believe they are quite living, or dead ones unwilling to believe they are quite dead. Their America is, consequently, neither earth nor heaven nor hell, but Limbo: a twilight landscape in which they can haunt only each other, being imperceptible to the wide-awake inhabitants of daylight America. They influence nothing, in fact, change nothing, want to change nothing in the land to which they have come as semisurvivors, not-quite ghosts. They do not vote, sign petitions, put on uniforms; they do not protest anything, cheer anything, join anything. Occasionally they go into business, dealing chiefly with each other; more frequently they write or lecture; always they make love, incestuously, of course, and tell stories, true or false, to those who speak their language. But especially, they hide—or get lost.

Lostness. It is the leitmotif, the compulsive theme of Singer's American tales. Especially his demi-autobiographical male protagonists, but by no means they alone, lose their wallets, their papers, their manuscripts (asserting the immortality of Yiddish), their keys, their way, themselves. They take the wrong trains, end up in the wrong hotels or the right ones on the wrong day. It seems to me apt, therefore, that Singer, for whose sake most of us, certainly I, were present in San Francisco, lost *us*—never making it to the meeting of the MLA group at which I delivered the first version of this paper.

But it is this theme which, paradoxically, makes him seem finally one of us, one more Stranger in a Strange Land; which is to say, one more American, as *Enemies, A Love Story,* his single novel set in the United States and published in English, makes abundantly clear—particularly in its last pages, where Singer actually loses Herman Broder, his main character. It seems at first glance the most astonishing, terrifying, and satisfactory thing about that eminently astonishing, terrifying, and satisfactory book. Yet it is clear from the first that no other fate can possibly await Broder except to vanish. He is by profession a ghost writer, but this means (as anyone who knows anything about Singer's narrative mode is aware) that he is a ghost who writes, as well as the author of works issued under someone else's name: not *symbolically* a ghost, let it be clear, but a ghost in all the superactuality of popular fiction.

Singer writes still in the unfallen world before the invention of *symbolisme*: a world in which the archetypes have not yet been introjected, but are still Out There with the rest of us. In his stories, therefore, metaphor is not generalized into symbol or allegory, as in the works of literary modernism, but specified in hallucinatory character and events, as in the fantasies of schizophrenics, or the best-selling fictions of Dickens, Conan Doyle, and the writers of daytime serials on television. For this reason, my barely literate grandfather could read him out of his daily newspaper, and my quite illiterate grandmother listen to him read aloud with as much pleasure and understanding (more, in one sense at least) as I.

Entangled throughout the course of the novel with competing wives or quasi-wives with equal claims, Herman Broder seems for a long time utterly unlike the typical American protagonist in flight from the world of women. Toward the end, however, he is tempted, much as Dimmesdale was tempted by Hester in *The Scarlet Letter*, to flee the complexities and conflicts his own lies have created for a romantic utopia à deux beyond the limits of law as he knows it. But if, again like Dimmesdale, he does not yield to that temptation, this is not because he has chosen to tell the truth and die, but because his Hester, who is called Masha, a hysterical survivor of the Holocaust, half Lilith and half Angel of Death, commits suicide at the last minute.

What ensues for Broder is not quite clear, for as I indicated earlier, he simply disappears from the final pages of the book; which is to say, Singer will not or cannot discern his ultimate fate. He leaves that task instead to one of the surviving wives, who speculates that her husband may have died, offstage, outside the fiction. It is too European an ending to bear; and I would prefer therefore to believe that he chose instead the truly American flight to total loneliness, an undefined territory ahead. If this makes him seem disconcertingly like Huckleberry Finn, that is fair enough in light of the fact that his strategy throughout the novel has been, not unlike Huck's, to "flee from evil, hide from danger, avoid showdowns."

And, after all, Singer himself suggests—or at least permits one of his characters to suggest—that maybe Herman is alive and hiding out in "an American version of his Polish hayloft": a reference that becomes clear when we remember that he had concealed himself under the hay in a peasant's barn throughout the whole of World War II, sleeping out the Holocaust, even as Rip Van Winkle had slept out the American Revolution. It occurs to me, moreover, that an American version of a Polish hayloft would be nothing more nor less than America itself: the Wilderness America of writers Singer has never read, like Melville and Twain, Hemingway and Faulkner, Mailer and Bellow—a mythic land as invisible to the other characters in Singer's novel as their world is to us, except in his pages, where improbably our boundaries meet.

Why Is the Grail Knight Jewish?
A *Passover Meditation*

O‌F all the legends, the communal dreams that have possessed the imagination of the West, that of the Grail seems the most tantalizing and evasive. It not merely remains—after eight hundred years of writing, rewriting, emendation, and commentary—contradictory, inchoate and incomplete; but it slips maddeningly through the fingers of all who strive to possess it. It belongs finally to no one and to everyone: the critic and scholar, the prophet, the priest and the politician as well as the poet, the sculptor, and the illustrator of children's books. Most of all, however, it belongs to the children who read such books or listen to them being read aloud—or merely look at the pictures—and have blessedly never heard of Chrétien de Troyes or Wolfram or the pseudo-Wauchier or Malory.

It is therefore in the voice of what survives in me of the child that I prefer to speak of the Grail: a child moved by wonder in the presence of a dream presumably first dreamed by others, but so like dreams he has already dreamed himself that he sometimes believed he had invented it; though, in fact, its wonder contained, as he somehow sensed from the start, a hint of terror, a threat.

At any rate, I feel committed to an attempt to redream that Passover dream as if it were my own; or to put it somewhat less metaphorically, to try to relocate the myth that exists before, after, outside all of the Christian texts that pretend to embody it, by demonstrating the sense in which it is a Jewish myth. Or perhaps I mean rather a myth about Jews: a reflection of the plight of my own people at a particular historical moment— recorded first by one who may have been a Jew converted to Christianity, and then revised by a score of gentiles, some more, some less aware of what in mythological terms they were doing. Think of Wolfram, for instance, who traced the ultimate origins of the myth to something the Jew Phlegetanis had read in the stars.

But how to locate the Myth of the Grail is the question, since like all myths it exists outside of any particular combination of words—exists first of all as an ever-expanding and changing set of magical names: Gawain and Perceval, Galahad and Bors, Joseph and Pelles and Bron. But also it pre-exists as a set of archetypal misadventures: the unasked question of the schle-miel son, the mysterious wound of the invisible father, the failed first quest and the inconclusive second chance. Ultimately, however, and primordially as well, the legend consists of a cluster of wordless images and icons, called by names no one quite understands, like *Grail* itself.

At first, even the number of the aboriginal icons was unsure, though it narrowed finally to four clearly defined symbols: cup and lance, sword and dish, which in turn became pips on playing cards, diamonds and clubs, hearts and spades, as the dream which became literature (though it aspired first perhaps to the status of scripture) ended as an amusement, a parlor game. But what does it all mean? we are driven to ask, having learned from the discomfiture of the schlemiel knight not to keep silent about such matters. Whom does the Grail serve?

For a long time we have teased ourselves with the notion that if only we could see it all—the total pattern, the gestalt, the completed tale with a proper beginning and end—we would know. But we possess only fragments, scraps, "a heap of testimony," which is in Hebrew *Galaad*, the final name of the many-named Grail knight. And at the beginning of it all there is the mysterious and contradictory poem of Chrétien de Troyes, the text of which hastens to assure us that it is not a beginning, that before it there was already a tradition written down in books, and which breaks off rather than concludes, presumably at the death of its author.

No wonder that the readers of Chrétien's fragmentary poem have most often felt it more challenging than satisfactory: an invitation to finish the tale and thus answer the questions it posed and left unanswered; or perhaps it would be better to say, using its own central metaphor, to find questions for the answers it left dangling. At any rate, almost immediately four or five poets, known and unknown, tried to finish the tale in Chrétien's own tongue; and before half a century had passed, there existed in prose and verse, in French and English and German, a half dozen major attempts to fill in the blanks, fore and aft, of a recorded dream, which perhaps by its very essence had to, has still to, blur away at the edges rather than be sharply focused.

Yet how hard it has proved for poets and scholars alike to accept the fact that, being in the deepest sense popular fiction, the Grail story has *necessarily* neither a proper Aristotelian beginning nor end, but only an indefinitely extensible middle, like a soap opera or a comic strip. Moreover, the attempt to end the essentially endless tale often, perhaps inevitably, implies a covert desire to capture it, use it, exploit it by euphemerizing or allegorizing its magic inconsequence in the interests of one cause or another: to promote the reform of monastic life, or to advertise a shrine, authenticate a relic, or support the bishops of Glastonbury against those of Canterbury; perhaps even to subvert the Roman Church by providing an alternative version of the apostolic succession and a new reading of Christ's symbolic transformation of the Passover seder.

Such acts of appropriation did not end with the Middle Ages. Nineteenth-century artists as different from each other as Wagner, Tennyson, and William Morris have reworked the legend on behalf of German naturalism, the sanctity of the bourgeois family and artsy-craftsy socialism. Moreover, in our own century, John Cowper Powys has sought to bend the myth to serve his own eccentric neo-Welsh mysticism, while Charles Williams has redeployed it in the interests of anti-Semitism, the polite occult and a genteel Anglicanism.

There has been one radical change in recent times, however, as, from the mid-nineteenth century, scholars began to contend with poets, artists, and priests for the right to complete, interpret, or appropriate the myth. Typically, however, such scholars have (as is the habit of their trade) attempted to complete it by looking *backward*, by finding the roots, the beginnings, something before Chrétien's eruption into print: if not that perhaps nonexistent book from the library of Philip of Flanders, to which he himself alludes, then a Celtic original, Welsh or Irish; at the very least some trace of a folk tale, some evidence of a prior religious rite or lapsed cult—*something*.

Diligent source-hunters have discovered presumable roots for the Grail legend in accounts of voyages to fairy land, in Greek mystery religions, the Jewish Kabbalah, the Byzantine rite, the ceremonies of the martyred Cathars, the rituals of freemasonry or of the Knights Templars, the cults of Attis and Adonis, and the worship of a burning glass as a symbol of the Holy Trinity. Sometimes the proponents of such theories have claimed to find survivals of such ancient cult practices in still living faiths ranging from Methodism to Rosicrucianism. Indeed, for the most literal-minded devotees of the myth, the physical Grail still exists (though this relic of a faith institutionalized only in literature has been variously portrayed as a stone, a platter, and a chalice) in regions as remote from each other as the Abbey at Glastonbury and the Castle of Montségur, to which I made pilgrimages before I realized that I, too, was engaged in the vainest and most alluring of quests. In that quest strange allies have gathered together, including—if *The Morning of the Magicians* can be believed—Adolf Hitler, who planned an expedition to recover it from a remote hiding place in Central Asia, revealed to him by one of his gurus, once the great war was won. But evoking the name of Hitler not only reminds us that the connection between anti-Semitism and the Grail has persisted from the start into our own time; but alerts us also to the fact that all seekers for the Grail tend to continue the story, imagining for it new endings as well as new beginnings.

Even the scholars, despite their primary interest in etiology, have become unworthy continuers of the legend, collaborators in the endless web of narrative the Western world never ceases to spin around its central icons. I refer not only to the sense in which all criticism implies a revision of the texts it pretends to explicate, or even to the way in which this is particularly true in the case of popular literature, to which in some deep sense the Grail story belongs. I refer chiefly to the specific case of Jessie Weston's *From Ritual to Romance*, the crowning work of a lifetime of Arthurian scholarship, which became an occasion for T. S. Eliot's *The Waste Land*, that key book of the modernist canon, which also evokes, via a tag from Verlaine, Wagner's reworking of the legend according to Wolfram von Eschenbach. Nor was that the end of the process; for if Eliot's poem connects back on the one hand to Weston's scholarly study, which it thus makes retrospectively also a work of literature, a continuation of Chrétien, on the other hand it connects forward to Bernard Malamud's allegorical fiction, *The Natural*. Is it merely paradoxical, then, that the most ambitious poem of an ex-American anti-Semite should have been the source for the only (apparently) non-Jewish novel of a Jewish-American author, who has ever since made Jewishness his central theme? Or did Malamud perceive somehow, on some level of awareness, the centrality of Jewishness to the original Grail story, which Eliot did not, and, indeed, could not, pledged as he was to ban the "perfidious Jews" ("freethinking Jews," he preferred to say) from his ideal commonwealth?

It is not, however, with the whole lifespan of the twice-born Grail legend that I am centrally concerned, though its death in the High Renaissance and its rebirth during the later stages of Romanticism is a subject I find fascinating and instructive. It is rather with the first fifty years of its first life, its infancy, or more properly, its early maturity, since it was born full-grown with Chrétien's *Perceval*. This means that I shall be dealing with the Grail legend primarily as a product of the "twelfth-century renaissance": a cultural phenomenon quite as characteristic of that postmillennial time as the invention of the university, the final fruition of scholasticism, the beginnings of modern urbanism, and the backlash of the failed Crusades, which had set out to reclaim the Holy Land and had ended by bringing back to Europe leprosy and anti-Semitism. The twelfth century marks, I am suggesting, the beginning of the end of tolerance or quasi-tolerance of the Jews, even in such communities as Troyes, where earlier they had moved freely, disputed openly, owned property, and functioned almost, *almost* as accepted members of the total community.

But the twelfth century was also the moment in which the institution we have come to call "literature" was first fully established. Vernacular poetry and prose dealing chiefly, or even exclusively, with secular concerns like war and love and imbued with values non- or even anti-Christian were barely a century old, when Chrétien wrote the narrative in which the images and themes of the Grail story surfaced for the first time. His language, his music, his tone were derived from those of the secular romances with which indeed he had experimented earlier; but his subject matter this time is, however ambiguously, religious though not quite orthodox. And I am, indeed, convinced that his otherwise inexplicably influential narrative is an attempt to represent, by way of the Grail Legend, a crisis not only in the troubled relationship of "literature" to "Scripture," but also of the Old Testament to the New, which is to say, of the surviving Jewish community in Europe to the Holy Roman Catholic Church.

For many years, I must confess, I was aware of only one half of the conflict reflected in the Grail story, that between the values imposed on the imperfectly Christianized pagans of Western Europe by a proselytizing faith, and those implicit in the Matter of Britain: that mass of story material neither Hellenic nor Hebraic, which had been released from the collective unconsciousness of Europe by the free fantasy permitted in the vulgar literatures. What I have become aware of only recently are the implications of that newly intensified conflict for the Jews, who were cast in the role of archetypal enemy twice over: not just as the killers of Christ, though they are, indeed, presented as such from Chrétien on, but also as the founders of Christianity, toward which nominally Christian Europeans continued for a long time (perhaps even as late as Hitler) to feel a profound ambivalence. That ambivalence they dared express only obliquely in the extrascriptural mythology, which stands at the very center of the Grail legend, about the transmission of the Christian faith to the westernmost reaches of Europe. I am referring, of course, to the oddly melancholy, the profoundly antitriumphal saga of Joseph of Arimathea and the long line of Jews who succeeded him as keepers of the Grail, right down to that oddly Jewish-non-Jewish son of a Jewish mother, Galahad. I was disturbed by the sadness of the Grail story even as it had descended to me in simplified and expurgated versions of Malory's *Morte d'Arthur*.

I did not understand that sadness, knowing only that though I loved the rest of the Arthurian story, I hated the Grail quest, and especially its anticlimax in the adventures of the disturbingly effete and maidenly Galahad, who had a vision but won the love of no lady. Like all other readers—I felt sure—my sympathies were with the resolute but faithful "sinner," Lancelot; and I did not understand why everyone did not stand up and declare that all had gone well until the intrusion of the Grail had turned upside down the values of a world which had until then seemed the world of my own dreams, indeed of the dreams of all boys, even an already scholarly and scared small Jew reading about the Round Table in Newark, New Jersey.

On my way toward a deeper understanding, I came first to see how the Grail story, though integrated into the Arthurian framework and in one sense inseparable from it, represented a set of values not merely alien but fatally hostile to the codes of chivalry and courtly love, which motivated Camelot—as alien and hostile as Jewish theocratic morality was to the ceremonial hedonism of the Celts. And the Grail itself—whether we understand it as the cup of the Passover benediction, the platter which held the paschal sacrifice, or the plate in which the unleavened bread was displayed—I came to see was a symbol for the role of Judaism in subverting the chivalric codes and a way of life dependent on them. Seen in this light the myth of the Grail figures forth the doom of a lovely imperfect civilization based on the poeticizing of carnal passion and bloodshed, and unable finally (though the myth itself represents a gallant attempt) to assimilate either Jewish law or the Jewish dream of a Messiah in its Nazarene form.

I was, I think, originally led astray by such interpretations of the Grail myth as Jessie Weston's, which in attempting to identify it with the myth of the dying and reborn God ended by falsifying it completely. We do not really experience or remember the Grail legend, in whatever text we encounter it, as a joyous tale, a high comedy ending with the healing of a king and the restoration of fertility to a wasteland, though, to be sure, its story line contains such elements.

Typically, the wounded king recovers only in order to die; and the Grail knight, the deliverer, more often than not does not reign over the world his achieved quest has redeemed, but retires, withdraws, disappears—taking with him into concealment the Grail itself. And his retirement leaves the world, as it were, doubly desolate, bereft of its chief talisman and its last hero. What is left after this double bereavement, which constitutes a kind of failed Second Coming, is neither nothingness nor a new heaven and a new earth—only the same old world (as I who read the story first in the *Morte d'Arthur* can never forget) without the Round Table, from which knights sallied forth to right its wrongs, and without the great adulterous love of Lancelot and Guinevere, which lightened for a little while its darkness. It seems a high price to pay for the redemption of a single saint in armor; and perhaps on some level the whole tale constitutes a criticism, more dreamed than formulated, of what the transplantation of the Judeo-Christian mythology had actually meant for the West: the salvation of a handful of individuals and the loss of a great secular glory.

In the most pathetic version of the tale, the point is especially clear. In order for the final Grail knight, Galahad, to be born the hitherto perfect warrior, Lancelot, befuddled by drink and magic, must betray his true beloved, for whom he initially betrayed his true king. It is in the bed of a Jewish girl that that final betrayal is accomplished, and in that same bed she gives birth to the Jewish son (descent according to Orthodox law being matrilineal) who is destined to defeat his goyish father.

How as a child I hated that moment of defeat—hated the downfall of the greatest knight in the world, the greatest lover at the hands of one who, though begotten in passion, never learned to love as a man loves, and was not of this world from the moment he entered it. And what would I have made of it all, I wonder now, if anyone had suggested to me then that in the encounter of Galahad and Lancelot were represented in allegory or projection the troubled nightmares occasioned by the transmission into Britain, the ultimate West, of a strange new morality and an even stranger messianic myth by way of the first Jew who ever landed on its shores.

All of this may seem remote from the tale as its first teller told it, remote from the ironic, only intermittently religious poem of Chrétien de Troyes. But it took only a half century or less for the Jewish lineage of the Grail knight (whether called Perceval or Galahad) to be clearly spelled out. And though Chrétien himself does not do so, he comes close toward the very end of the last Perceval episode in his poem—at the same point, in fact, when a presumably unmotivated anti-Semitic aside gives us pause, suggesting, if we do not too quickly dismiss it, that the Jews, the Jewish "problem," the Dispute of Church and Synagogue, the Mystery of Israel as first defined by St.

Paul, is somehow in the back of the poet's mind, if not at the center of his concern.

At first, however, Chrétien does not seem to know where he is going, or perhaps is determined to mislead his auditors. Certainly, his tone is initially mocking, reflecting a kind of courtly condescension (not unlike that in Perrault's much later rendition of similar folk material) toward the Breton-Welsh, Irish material he is reworking, stuff of remotely bardic origin, perhaps, but more recently transmitted and transformed by unlettered peasants.

In any event, he seems to have felt a need to treat his material in a style we have come only recently to call "camp," though the practice is an ancient one—a way of coming to terms with stories for which one is ashamed to admit his secret love, by pretending to burlesque them.

Especially in the Perceval sections of his narrative, Chrétien employs this hypocritical device. The other half of his split hero, Gawain, is a courtly figure sharing fully the vices and virtues of the poet's original aristocratic audience, and therefore he does not really demand such treatment. But Perceval is from the start an outsider not only because he is a Welshman, which is to say, a stranger from the woods, but because he is a naif without a name, a muddleheaded mama's boy unsocialized by contact with older, more experienced male models. No wonder he cannot tell an armed knight from an angelic messenger, and is constantly getting into trouble by using yesterday's good advice today. It is a standard comic device in put-down tales told by the sophisticated at the expense of ethnic or class outsiders.

Yet Perceval is finally transformed from an inarticulate schlemiel, a prefiguration of that son mentioned in the Passover seder, who is "unable even to ask," to a kind of hero—if not quite a tragic hero, at least a disturbingly problematical figure. But his transformation occurs inadvertently, by mistake, as it were, when, without knowing what he is doing, he manages to kill his mother by the simple process of leaving home. It is like an old Jewish joke actualized into terror, the conventional threat of the Jewish mother ("Believe me, my son, if you go away from me, I'll drop dead!") become fact.

But the threat fulfilled means the transformation of Perceval's mother from a kind of Mrs. Portnoy *ante littera* into the archetypal mother of us all, Rachel who weeps for her children and will not be comforted. And by the same token, it means the metamorphosis of a naive runaway boy into a kind of anti- or counter-Oedipus. Twice over Perceval is told (to the annoyance, I gather, of some scholars) that his inability to ask the proper question at the proper moment is due to his guilt for having, however unwillingly, slain his mother. But the two events, I am convinced, are tied together, not accidentally but necessarily, which is to say, structurally, mythologically, archetypally; since the mystery of an answer-without-a-question is associated with mother-murder even as the question-without-an-answer (the riddle of the Sphinx) is with father-murder.

What I am suggesting has been suggested several times before, most notably by the eminent French anthropologist Claude Lévi-Strauss in his inaugural address at the Collège de France. And it seems apt that it be a Jewish prophet once more who has most convincingly argued that the Grail legend is the complement, the binary opposite of the story of Oedipus, the Jewish antithesis to a Greek thesis. What is evoked is incest avoided rather than achieved; for as Lévi-Strauss goes on to explain of the Oedipus myth, "between the puzzle solution and incest there exists a relationship. Like the solved puzzle, incest brings together elements doomed to remain separate." The unsolved puzzle, on the other hand, betokens the maintaining of that separation. Ironically, however, it can only reverse the tragic oedipal denouement, not resolve it comically.

The mother, fled from, dies and the father is resurrected, or at least restored to sexual potency—but only if the question is asked to complete the riddle whose answer pre-exists. It is a Judeo-Christian paradox based on a Jewish joke. In light of all this, it is especially fitting that Chrétien's hero end up in the Grail castle, an oddly displaced replica of the Temple of the Jews, as scholars have been pointing out ever since Moses Gaster. Moreover, within its walls, a transmogrified Passover seder is being enacted in Orthodox Jewish style: the plate of the paschal sacrifice lifted aloft, the candles lit, the stage set in fact for the youngest male present, who is Perceval, to ask the traditional question, which of course he does not. So pure is he, so uninitiated, so sexually ignorant that he cannot even ask, like the Simple Son of the Paschal Haggadah, *"mah zeh?"*— what is it? And so the springtime, whose coming is celebrated at the most literal level of the allegorical Passover ritual, never arrives. What is endured instead is what Lévi-Strauss calls "an eternal winter . . . pure to the point of sterility"—the baleful opposite of the Theban "eternal summer . . . licentious to the point of sterility."

The implication of Perceval's failure seems to me clear, though Chrétien apparently did not feel the necessity of spelling it out. If the virgin quester had asked at the failed seder "Whom does the Grail serve?"; or if he were to be given a second chance and ask it at last, what he would have been or would be told is what is always told when the ritual question is asked, and "the periodicity of the seasonal rhythm" delivered from ascetic restraints without being permitted to lapse into orgiastic excess. It is the past on which the living feed in order to produce the yet unborn who will feed them by ritual remembrance. But this means in a Christian poem of the late Middle Ages that the seeker for a Second Coming will be told that the Grail serves the wounded old man in the farther room, who, though sterile, now, is the quester's own ancestor, which is to say, a Jewish patriarch. And the whole transaction symbolizes what is otherwise figured forth in the giving of manna: a sign that even in the desert, the Wasteland, God feeds his Chosen People. Not them alone, however, as the Passover seder reminds us, opening as it does with the cry: "Let those who are hungry come in and eat." But them first of all—and the others, the gentiles, only through them, their election and their casting away, which extends but does not annul the Promise sealed with the circumcision.

In Chrétien's poem, Perceval learns that he is descended from the rich Fisher King through the mother he denied and killed; but it is not made explicit that this archetypal, undying male ancestor is himself Jewish. For that, the legend of Joseph of Arimathea, the Jewish refugee who bore the relics of the crucifixion to the West, had to be interwoven with the other strands of the tale. And in the process the sacrificial platter assumed yet one more level of significance, being transformed into the kiddush cup of the Last Supper, without losing its other ceremonial meanings. But this has already been accomplished by the time of the First Continuation of Chrétien's unfinished poem, at least in a passage considered by some to be an interpolation in the text. It is here that we first read how Joseph of Arimathea, after, like any good Jew, blowing a horn and ceremoniously washing his hands, sits down to the feast provided by the Grail. And when it is finished, we are told that he prays to God that neither glory nor the Grail pass from his line. "And," the author continues, "thus it befell. . . . For after Joseph's death no man had possession of it unless he was of Joseph's lineage. In truth the Rich Fisher descended from him, and all his heirs, and, they say, Guillem Guenelaus and his son Perceval."

From then on the tradition of the Jewishness of the Grail

knight was set; nor is it disturbed when Perceval is replaced at the center of the story by Galahad. As a matter of fact, the mythological ante is raised by the switch, since in Galahad's case the Jewish roots of the Grail knight are extended even farther back along the messianic line of descent; so that in the *Queste de Sangraal* Galahad is described on his first arrival at Arthur's Court not merely as one "of King's lineage and of the kindred of Joseph of Arimathea," but also as "the desired Knight who is descended from high lineage of King David."

But why, one is drawn to ask, this palpable effort twelve hundred years after Christ to remythologize the Last Supper, to reinvent the *Meshiach ben David*, to reimagine the mission of the Jews in the gentile world? The clue is, I think, to be found in a passage to which I have already alluded, and which has always troubled me especially because it is so essential a part of the nearest thing to a true conclusion to Chrétien's account of Perceval: an immediate prologue to his taking Easter Communion and his dismissal with the tantalizing phrase, "of him the tale tells no more." After a series of misadventures, beginning with the fiasco in the Grail castle, that not-quite-hero had lapsed, according to this account, into a state of unawareness more abysmal than his first stupidity. So total is his amnesia, his unlearning of the difficult lessons he has so perilously learned, that he is found wandering abroad fully armed on Good Friday, accoutred for bloodshed like "the Jews and the sinners who slew" Christ on that day. Indeed, a knight who encounters him by chance is so outraged at his gross behavior that he cries out in reproach, "Dear good sir, do you not believe in Jesus Christ, who wrote the New Law and gave it to the Christians. . . ? The wicked Jews, whom one should kill like dogs, wrought their own harm and our good when they raised him to the cross. Themselves they destroyed, and us they saved." It is a blood-chilling phrase, spoken presumably on behalf of one who had preached the forgiveness of our enemies, "whom one should kill like dogs."

Actually, Chrétien has earlier praised, in the prologue to his poem, the supreme Christian virtue of charity, and some latter-day scholars have even insisted that this is the central theme of the work. But there is little enough charity displayed in this gratuitous incitement to a pogrom, this encapsulated but virulent version of the Mystery of Israel: the paradox that the salvation of the gentiles was achieved only at the price of the casting away of the Jews, which seems, on the face of it, a special occasion for that virtue.

Chrétien might well have read only shortly before, as Urban T. Holmes has reminded us, the seventy-ninth sermon of St. Bernard on the subject, of which there was a copy in the library of his patron Philip. Indeed, the notion of Israel as the "mother" of Christianity may have come to him from that source, but he did not respond to its plea for understanding and tolerance. "The great charity of the Church," Bernard preached, "does not wish to withhold its delights from the rival Synagogue. . . . This is marvellous, that salvation is from the Jews. The Saviour has returned to the place whence He came for that the remnants of Israel may be saved. The branches are not ungrateful to the root, nor the sons to the mother . . . and thus all of Israel may be saved."

This is, of course (except for the mother-son metaphor), standard Pauline doctrine as argued in the *Epistle to the Hebrews*, Chapter 11, but Christian Europe needed to be reminded of it in the twelfth century; for even as Chrétien was writing, Jewish refugees were flocking into Troyes from outlying small towns, where rioting Christians were in fact threatening to "kill them like dogs." Among those refugees was the grandson of Rashi, eminent rabbi and commentator on the Scriptures, who two generations before had made Chrétien's native city a center of

Jewish learning, in some sense a Jewish city. There are some who argue that Chrétien had himself been born a Jew; and indeed his name is one frequently given to converts. But there is no conclusive evidence and finally that issue is of small importance, since in any case he must have known Jews, exchanged greetings with them, perhaps conversed and argued with them. And certainly he could not have been ignorant of the growing terror that threatened them in his native place.

Indeed his poem reflects at its deepest levels, at precisely those places where personal anguish and religious commitment break through his defensive irony and courtly condescension, an awareness of that crisis. It is not just an explosion of hatred which concludes the Perceval episode of his poem, though it is that also; but a confession as well of the guilt bred by the long internecine struggle of Christians and Jews over which were the true Grail bearers, the authentic continuers of the tradition and inheritors of the Promise. If, as Chrétien suggests, mythologically, archetypally speaking, all Jews are guilty of deicide, all Christians, as Bernard implies, are inadvertent matricides simply for having abandoned the Synagogue, and they compound their primal crime by murdering, or advocating the murder of those who still remain faithful to the maternal cult. Having thus killed Rachel, they are forever impotent, capable perhaps of imagining the ultimate mystery, of seeing in the mind's eye the Grail, borne typically in the legend, I remind you, by a woman, who represents typically, I suggest, what is feminine in the Divine, the Great Mother: but not of touching it, possessing it—being fed by it as the child is fed at the maternal breast.

In Chrétien's version of the story, there is no Galahad—no second Savior, who kills his gentile father to avenge his Jewish mother, and, completing the ritual, sees the Grail that has kept alive his maternal male ancestors. In any case, that Second

Savior saves nothing and feeds no one but himself, incapable of fertilizing the world with his icy virginity, so that finally he symbolizes a Second Coming even more inconclusive than the first. This later version of the Grail story is, however desperate, at least a Christian fable; Chrétien's earlier account takes from Christianity chiefly its anti-Jewishness, remaining an elegy for Celtic myth and courtly values with anti-Semitic overtones, the saddest, perhaps, of all comic poems. But it is fitting, after all, that a work which ended by denying a charity it had begun by evoking, denying it specifically to God's Chosen People, and thus contributing in its own small way to the centuries of persecution that lay ahead for the Jews of Europe, should, at its most memorable moments, be a poem about failure: the tragicomic failure of the goyim to live by the code they had learned first from Israel, and with which, to speak the truth, they have not yet come to terms.

Styron's Choice

MANY years ago I vowed that not only would I never write about Hitler's extermination camps, but that I would not even write in response to those who did. Certainly, I told myself, I would never be foolish enough to enter into the argument, which finds most Jews on one side, most gentiles on the other, about whether what occurred in those camps is best understood as a monstrous climax to the millennial war of paganism against Judaism, or an episode in the eternal human struggle between good and evil. Once, I must confess, I broke my vow of silence: I was tempted in 1950, for reasons I no longer clearly remember, to review John Hersey's *The Wall*, which I ended up condemning for having dared reduce the mystery of the attempted destruction of Jewry to a handful of comfortably familiar, or as I then called them, "Christian" platitudes. It was so ill-tempered a piece that it offended everyone, Jew and gentile alike, and was finally not printed, occasioning

me much distress. But in retrospect it seems to me *right* that
I should have been forced into the silence I was not wise enough
to keep.

Yet now again I find myself trying to deal with a book about
the Holocaust by an American goy, the epigraphs to which
(extracted from Rilke and Malraux) make clear that for its author
Auschwitz signifies a pair of abstractions: the Slaughter of Children and the conflict between Fraternity and Absolute Evil.
Even as I write these words, however, I hear echoing in my
head (it is the season of Passover) verses from the Haggadah:
"for not only one hath risen up against us, but in every generation there are some who rise up against us, to annihilate
us . . .", ironically counterpointing a text that insists that gypsies
also died in the ovens, along with anti-Semitic Poles, and argues
that, after all, the plight of Hitler's victims was not so utterly
different from that of slaves in Styron's ancestral South. The
Holocaust, which haunts us both, separates rather than joins
us—though comically, thank God, rather than tragically; which
is to say, we two American men of letters are fighting out a
harmless, parodic version of the conflict that elsewhere, else-
when, debouched in Auschwitz. And it is my sense that Styron
is aware of this, that his book is in large part about it, which
has emboldened me to continue this dialogue with him, to play,
as it were, Shean to his Gallagher.

Why else has he set a novel, about a Polish survivor of Auschwitz and her execution, in the United States of 1947 (as remembered thirty years later), a world and time about which
both of us can speak without pretension, as we cannot about
the gas chambers of 1941? The book includes, to be sure, "historical" passages about the camps, which verge on the kind of
horror pornography and easy pathos that seem inseparable from
the subject and may, indeed, make it a best-seller. But such
scenes are for me only redeemed by being reported secondhand,

through that Polish woman, who is portrayed as a compulsive liar. They are contained, moreover, within an autobiographical frame that ironizes bathos and pathos alike, by reminding us that the novel we are reading, whatever else it may be about, is *also* about the burlesque struggle (that for Styron's generation and mine loomed so large) over who was to become the laureate of late twentieth-century America, the urban Jew or the Southern WASP?

That struggle is, of course, now over, the final victory of the Jews signaled by the award of the Nobel Prize to Saul Bellow, as all but predicted in 1947 by Nathan Landau, the first New York Jew whom Stingo, the book's Southern Presbyterian narrator, comes really to know. "Southern writing as a force is going to be over in a few years," Nathan announces. "Jewish writing is going to be the important force. . . ." When challenged to give an example, he names Bellow, leaving Stingo, whose life history is identical to Styron's own, with a terrified vision of himself "running a pale tenth in the literary track race," eating "the dust of a pounding fast-footed horde of Bellows and Schwartzes and Levys and Mandelbaums."

From the start, Styron had used mouthpieces not unlike himself; but he did not hit upon the device of making his own writing career an essential part of his spokesman's prehistory until *The Way of a Warrior*, a selection from which appeared in the September 1971 *Esquire*. In that novel (since abandoned or postponed) Styron carries the account of his battle with Bellow up to 1951, reprinting a somewhat snide first review of his *Lie Down in Darkness*, signed only by initial, which his not-quite-fictional surrogate speculates must belong to "a hater of Southerners . . . a C.C.N.Y. type with . . . piles, and joyless Talmudic eyes, probably teaching . . . muddy wisdom about Bellow, Malamud, and the Jewish renaissance." Ironically, however, it is such Talmudic types who made Styron's reputation, and continue to tout him (the last description of him as a "great writer" that I have seen was written by Irving Malin, who in fact teaches at City College), in a time when younger readers and writers seldom read him except as a class assignment— turning by preference to what Styron calls, a little bitterly, "cult" figures, from J. D. Salinger to Kurt Vonnegut, Jr.

Yet not so long ago he was considered even by eminent fellow writers like Norman Mailer a contender for the title still held by Ernest Hemingway. And why he has faded in the stretch is hard to say. In part, perhaps, because he has not published often enough to remain fully visible, even those Jewish-American literary mavens who annually nominate, along with a list of largely Jewish-American favorites, a "White Hope," a WASP worthy of mention alongside of Bellow and Malamud, have switched from Styron to Wright Morris or Truman Capote or John Barth or John Updike. Moreover, Styron's second big book, *Set This House on Fire*, bombed badly, turning off even the kind of critic who had originally hailed his espousal of "high style" as a welcome relief from the lumpen prose of "realists" like James Jones, but who now became uncomfortably aware that his relentless overwriting owed more to the example of Thomas Wolfe than that of James Joyce.

Many of them were, therefore, reluctant to come to his defense against the scorn heaped on his next book. *The Confessions of Nat Turner* offended black nationalists and Jewish-American social scientists, jealous of his invasion of a "historical" territory they considered theirs by virtue of a prior claim and superior political insight. Indeed, to such critics the fact that this novel made it onto the best-seller lists and won for him the Pulitzer Prize seemed further proof that he had never really belonged in the realm of "high literature." I, on the other hand, was deeply moved by his work for the first time—impressed by the sheer chutzpah of the attempt. Picking up *Sophie's Choice,* therefore, I found myself hoping that he had not in the intervening years lost his nerve. I am delighted to report that, in fact, he has moved on to a subject considered by embattled Jews as untouchable by an outsider as slave rebellion had seemed to black militants in the late sixties—a subject, moreover, that Saul Bellow had already confronted in *Mr. Sammler's Planet.*

This time, however, Styron has not tried to tell his story of ultimate atrocity from inside the consciousness of a tragic and alien victim, as he did in *The Confessions of Nat Turner,* but has assumed instead the voice of the comic outsider he really is: an "ineffectual and horny" Calvinist, dreaming his first novel and his first lay in the midst of strangers whom he lusts for and fears, loves and hates. Only once before had a writer of comparable ambition and talent attempted to tender the plight of "the lonesome young Southerner amid the Kingdom of the Jews." This was, of course, Thomas Wolfe, whom Stingo tells us was a favorite of his and his mother's; and, as he does not confess, also of the Nazis. Styron is aware, however, as Wolfe was not, of the absurdity of the view of Jewish women that kindled the youthful eros of his mother and his younger self— enabling him to write what is for me the hilarious high-point of the book: a description of the failed seduction of a Brooklyn cockteaser called Leslie Lapidus, from which Stingo flees rigid, baffled, and enraged.

Oddly enough, in a novel centrally concerned with a historic crisis of Jewry, the only other Jew fully portrayed is Nathan Landau, a superarticulate psychotic and speed-freak, possessed in his manic phases by a hysterical hatred of all Germans, Poles, and Southern WASPs; as well as the baseless conviction that he is on the verge of a scientific breakthrough more important than the invention of the Salk vaccine or the discovery of penicillin. But he, like Leslie, is an American Jew, to whom

Auschwitz is as "fictional" as it is to Stingo. The European Jews who actually suffered and died in the camps remain shadowy figures reconstructed after considerable research in published accounts by survivors; while the two characters out of Auschwitz portrayed convincingly and in depth are both gentiles: Rudolph Höss and Sophie Zawistowska. But Höss belongs to "history," his name already familiar to us from the testimony at the Nuremburg Trials, the trial of Adolf Eichmann, and his own autobiography, which before Styron drew on it had already been fictionalized by the French novelist, Robert Merle. We know therefore before we begin that he was the commandant at Auschwitz for two years and that after Hitler's defeat he was tried and hanged amidst its rubble. Of Sophie in Auschwitz, on the other hand, we know only what Styron tells us—or rather what Stingo tells us she told him: that she had attempted to seduce Höss (to save one of her children) and failed; that her father and husband had died at the hands of the Nazis, in spite of their own homegrown Polish anti-Semitism; and that—final twist of irony—she was a habitual liar. To compound that irony, we are reminded that Höss, alone among the Nazis who lived to testify in public, *never lied*—subterfuge being as alien to him as personal sadism.

In the present time of the book, however, it is not Auschwitz that concerns us but its tragicomic aftermath: the ambivalent relationship of Sophie and Nathan, joined by guilt as well as passion—the guilt of a gentile survivor of the camps who has, however ineffectively, collaborated with the Nazis, and that of an American-Jewish outsider who, however unwillingly, was never there. This is reported to us directly by Stingo, a peeper, like Hawthorne's Miles Coverdale, at the coupling of others, and also like him, quite reliable, though impotent. Even when, by becoming Sophie's lover, Stingo manages to participate in the action, he proves incapable of influencing its outcome. The events he watches move inexorably not toward the happy ending of a marriage to Sophie, which would join him also to his beloved and hated Nathan, but to the death of both. Yet if this, too, is an American travesty of what happened at Auschwitz, unlike the contest of the Jewish and gentile writer, it baffles easy laughter.

No more, however, can it be responded to with easy tears. Only the blackest of gallows humor seems adequate to so inverted a parody of Jewish/gentile relations, in which the Jew becomes the victimizer and the gentile the victim: Nathan, identifying Sophie with the torturers of his people (and who is to say he is entirely wrong?), beats and kicks her, pisses on her, forces her to blow him, rapes her brutally, and at last seduces her into mutual suicide. But not before Sophie has escaped his influence long enough to join with Stingo in a litany of anti-Semitic abuse. "Jews," Sophie says, "God, how I hate them! Oh, the lies I have told you, Stingo . . . All my childhood, all my life I really hated Jews. They deserved it, this hate . . ." And when she concludes, "Nathan had everything that is bad in Jews . . . nothing of the little bit that's good," Stingo answers, "What's good about Jews at *all?*"

To be sure, Sophie returns to death in the arms of her Jewish lover, and Styron from the vantage point of thirty years later mocks Stingo's callow response; but to have revealed thus the dark ambivalence that underlies both his youthful obsession with Jews and his present resolve to make of the direst calamity the occasion for a "great novel" requires wit and courage as well as ambition. Had he proved just a little less ambitious, a little more witty and courageous, he might have been able to see the whole story as a joke not just on Stingo but on the unredeemably innocent culture that bred him; ending with the anti-climactic funeral sermon delivered over the bodies of Sophie and Nathan by a "synthetically serene" Unitarian Universalist preacher, who evokes the irrelevant holy names of Lincoln, Ralph Waldo Emerson, Dale Carnegie, Spinoza, Thomas Edison, and Sigmund Freud, while a "whining Hammond organ" plays Gounod's "Ave Maria."

Styron, however, is not able to leave it at that (and it is perhaps a final joke on me that I object, wanting somehow to make the book my own), going on to evoke *his* irrelevant names, Lao-Tzu, Jesus, Gautama Buddha, and *his* inadequate banalities: "Let your love flow out on all living things." And he closes, without irony, on some verses of Stingo—" 'Neath cold sand I dreamed of death/but woke at dawn to see/in glory, the bright, the morning star"—though they reflect not joy at the miraculous persistence of Israel, or even the triumph of Fraternity over Absolute Evil, but only the writer's selfish pleasure that one at least has lived to tell the tale, and it is he.

Going for the Long Ball

THE publication of the Big Novel that Norman Mailer has been promising for a quarter of a century now—"one that would require the seat of a Zola and the mind of a Joyce to do it properly"—seems to me an occasion for both celebration and dismay. On the one hand, it would be churlish not to cheer that long-awaited event, which, I must confess, I feel to be a long-deferred consummation for everyone who, like me, has read Mailer from the start of his career. On the other hand, I find its appearance profoundly disturbing, for I suddenly realize that the central pathos, the basic appeal of everything else Mailer has written, has come to depend on the fact that it was not yet that surely unwritable masterpiece that, in his own words, "Dostoyevsky and Marx; Joyce and Freud; Stendhal, Tolstoy, Proust, and Spengler; Faulkner and even . . . Hemingway might come to read, for it would carry what they had to tell another part of the way." For the last fourteen years, in fact, Mailer has published nothing at all that can truly be classified as a novel, and in the fourteen before that only two, *An American Dream* (1965) and *Why Are We in Vietnam?* (1967), the second of which seems in retrospect a tormented valedictory to the genre, a stuttering away into silence.

Yet somehow I have never been quite able to cease thinking of Mailer as a novelist. In part, surely, because he burst onto the scene in that guise: the wunderkind from Harvard and the battlefields of the Pacific who managed to please both critics and the mass audience with the first successful novel about what we hoped would be the last World War. It is not a book that has worn well, *The Naked and the Dead*, but never mind; implicit in it is an image that has survived: the image of the novelist who will someday do considerably better, perhaps best of all. And that image was reinforced rather than undercut by the failure of the two books that followed, *Barbary Shore* (1951) and *The Deer Park* (1955). The latter, indeed, represents what Mailer was able to salvage from the wreckage of his initial attempt at the Big Novel, projected at that point as a fiction in eight volumes, to which he was prepared to devote the next fifteen years of his life.

That supernovel, he tells us, was to deal with the adventures in the world of "communism . . . crime, homosexuality, and mysticism" of a kind of urbanized Hemingway hero called Sergius O'Shaugnessy: a superstud, superjock, and, of course, a mythic goy, dreamed by a little Jew called Sam Slovoda, "a small, frustrated man, a minor artist manqué." But Sam embodied a comic-pathetic version of Mailer himself that foredoomed his intendedly heroic venture. He kept wrestling with it for at least five years, referring to it still as "the new novel" in *Advertisements for Myself* (1959), in which he gathered together fragments of his compulsive rewriting of the earlier book, plus spin-off Sam/Sergius stories like "The Time of Her Time" and "The Man Who Studied Yoga." Nonetheless, though the Sergius in Mailer continues to speak still of his resolve "within ten years to hit the longest ball ever to go up into the air . . . of our American letters," the Sam in him is driven to confess that "I do not have the confidence that you will see it in its completed form."

Behind the manifold masks of the man who picketed the Pentagon or stabbed his own wife or helped release a murderer into our midst, there somehow had persisted the unchanging image of the onetime author of best-sellers who no longer writes novels at all, but will someday produce the greatest long fiction of the age. Or perhaps even more heroically, will die before it is done. Indeed, it scarcely seemed to matter which, as long as that promised book remained a fact of fiction rather than of life; which is to say, itself a myth, realer than real.

But suddenly, embarrassingly, the myth is here on my desk: *Ancient Evenings*, which traces the lives of Menenhetet, reincarnated as charioteer, general, harem master, and high priest in the nineteenth and twentieth Egyptian dynasties.

It should surprise no one, in any case, to find Mailer even in his Big Book adapting to his own uses a popular subgenre already invented by others. In this respect at least, he was never a pioneer, as is attested by his adaptation of the Anti-War Novel in *The Naked and the Dead*, the Hollywood Novel in *The Deer Park*, and the Hunt-as-Initiation Novel in *Why Are We in Vietnam?* Typically, however, Mailer has used his elders as models, rather than—as this time—the young, to whom he turns not merely for the form of *Ancient Evenings*, but for its main themes and motifs: polytheism, ritual cannibalism, righteous sadism, unwitting misogyny, sacramental sex, and especially pop occultism, including reincarnation, telepathy, even the not-quite-

reputable theory of the "two brains." All the standard para-
phernalia of neo-paganism—along with one of its favorite re-
discovered scriptures, the Egyptian Book of the Dead.

But at a deeper level, the return to Egypt becomes for Mailer
a deliberate inversion of the myth of the exodus—in which he
is able to project once more his lifelong fantasy of becoming the
"golden goy," as his surrogate, Menenhetet, rises by his own
wit and courage to sit at the right hand of a king who is also a
god, and makes it into the bed of his wife. The Egypt, moreover,
in which Menenhetet becomes rich and famous is an Egypt in
which Moses is demoted to the status of a second-rate magician,
who slips across the border under cover of night with a handful
of fellow slaves, but never challenges either Pharaoh or his
Gods. A world, that is to say, out of which Judaism never
emerges triumphant, so that in its alternate future Sam Slovoda
will never be born.

In Mailer's deeper imagination, however, Egypt represents
not merely the world without an exodus, but the anus (as Israel
does the penis, he had written earlier, and Africa the nose).
And in it, therefore, the ultimate expression of power is anal
rape. Indeed, before this book is over, the half-waking reverie
with which it begins turns into a deep-sleep nightmare, in which
Menenhetet is not merely betrayed but buggered by the Pharaoh he loves. It is a consummation with which Mailer has flirted
throughout his career—approaching it and retreating in *The
Naked and the Dead, An American Dream,* and finally *Why Are
We in Vietnam?*

Perhaps, however, not until he could manage to portray that
brutal consummation in the flesh could Mailer consummate his
other long-frustrated macho desire to write the Big One, to hit
the ball out of the park. In any event, in *Ancient Evenings* he
is able to portray twice over the consummation/degradation he
had so long repressed. Not only is Menenhetet anally raped by

his God-King, but in turn he himself rapes, orally this time, his own grandson, who bears his name and is the central narrator of the book—not, however, until they are both corpses, the one doomed to a second death, the other struggling to be reborn. It is as if at the heart of his ultimate fantasy Mailer wanted to imagine a single act that transgressed all the laws of Israel —against homosexuality, rape, incest, and necrophilia. And he goes on to detail it all with such relish, it is hard not to suspect that he wants his Big Novel to be yet one more goyish transgression: just such "an unpublishable book" as he had predicted in 1959, "an outlaw of the underground."

But the final ironies of his work are always beyond an author's conscious control. Even as I write this, I look down on Mailer's face, beaming up at me in triumph from the covers of *New York* and *Harvard Magazine,* and I read that 100,000 copies of *Ancient Evenings* have been sold before publication. But this, too, he must have desired—as indeed, I realize, I have, too.

Growing Up Post-Jewish

I MUST confess that my aging Jewish comedian's heart skipped a beat when I read the jacket blurb describing a book written by someone under forty as "the most important comic-Jewish novel since *Portnoy's Complaint*" (a summary that goes to the heart of the novel's anxieties, even though the blurb has disappeared from the final version). Scarcely any writers of that age who seem in any sense "important" these days are Jews. Indeed, I have long since decided that the Jewish-American novel is over and done with, a part of history rather than a living literature. To be sure, many of the Jewish-American authors whose newest work we used to await so breathlessly only a decade ago are still alive and writing. Moreover, they continue to be honored with prestigious awards, memorialized in adulatory biographies, and mined for quotations on Ph.D. examinations. In part for this very reason, however, their most recent books have come to seem not merely irrelevant but posthumous. In any case, from the start the Jewishness of such laureates of Jewish-American life was already vestigial, and their exploitation of it has come to seem in retrospect a final act of assimilation into the homogenized, postethnic society that made them rich and famous. It was perhaps an awareness of this that impelled Saul Bellow to make the fictional alter ego of *The Dean's December* not even a vestigial Jew but a goy.

How is it possible then, I asked myself, picking up *The Great Pretender* by James Atlas, to make an authentically Jewish comedy out of an account of the growing up of Ben Janis, the assimilated son of an already totally secularized ex-Jewish family, who passes from his suburban high school and a summer stint as a subeditor of *Poetry* magazine, via Harvard and Oxford and various unsatisfactory erotic adventures, to a good job at *Time*—dreaming all the while, to be sure, of becoming a Great Poet. This is funny enough, in fact, but not *Jewish* funny; which is to say, not quite as funny as such comic minor masterpieces of the Jewish-American Golden Age as Wallace Markfield's *To an Early Grave* or *A Mother's Kisses* by Bruce Jay Friedman. James Atlas's autobiographical first novel (the career of its protagonist is scarcely distinguishable from its author's) is, moreover, undercut throughout by a kind of covert self-pity and self-adulation reminiscent of James Joyce's *Portrait of the Artist as a Young Man*, clearly the chief model for this latter-day manifesto of a writer intent on forging in the smithy of his soul the uncreated conscience of his race. But what *race?* one is tempted to ask of Mr. Atlas, as one is not of Joyce.

It is, in any event, the "Jewishness" of this book which remains for me problematical—all the more so because it is not felt by its writer as a problem, although it is a pervasive issue. Symptomatically, the words *Jew* and *Jewish* appear rarely on its pages, and the word *gentile*, I think, never; certainly not

shikse or *goy*, the pejorative names by which the alien other—
despised or desired—is called in the ancestral mother tongue.
There are, it is true, a handful of Yiddish words scattered
through the novel, ranging from the endearment *boychick*, to
pupik, meaning bellybutton, and of course *tsuris*, meaning trouble. But there are quite as many words in Russian and even
more in French.

The only two characters specifically identified as "Jewish" are
Ben's two grandmothers, about whom he writes bad poems for
his classes in creative writing, and with the evocation of whom
his narrative opens and closes. The last words we hear from
one of those grandmothers in the book's final chapter, however,
are Russian: a passage from Pushkin that she reads aloud from
a volume Ben has brought to her in the nursing home where
she has come to die. Even in the Old World, and at a remove
of two generations, Ben's family has already been assimilated
into gentile culture. To be sure, in the first scene, which describes a grimly secular funeral service for his other grandmother, "a few words in Hebrew" are spoken. But they are not
reported, and in any case they are spoken by a lay friend of the
family. No rabbis allowed. (Was there no Kaddish, the traditional Jewish prayer for the dead?)

There are, indeed, no descriptions of any Jewish rites, no
celebrations of any Holy Days no matter how high. Nothing in
the past is denied, only forgotten in a kind of total amnesia.
Though there are peripheral passing mentions of pogroms in
Russia and the annihilation of European Jewry under the Nazis,
neither event resonates in Ben's deep psyche, any more than
does the Zionist dream of a return to Israel. Scarcely surprising,
then, that the fact or even the possibility of anti-Semitism in
his own America never occurs to the overprivileged Ben. He
is immune even to the vestigial paranoia that haunted the Jewish-American writers of the Golden Age, guilt-ridden and fear-

ful, even as they were invited into a world for so long considered *trayf*, taboo.

Yet the novel and its author (whose first book was *Delmore Schwartz: The Life of an American Poet*) are haunted by the specters of those somehow still Jewish predecessors: Saul Bellow, Isaac Rosenfeld, Lionel Trilling, Alfred Kazin, Irving Howe, George Steiner. Their names are evoked, however, side by side with those of eminent gentile intellectuals and artists like Mary McCarthy, Dwight MacDonald, and especially Robert Lowell, to whom, under a transparent pseudonym, Mr. Atlas devotes one of the most hilarious and heartbreaking passages of the book. These are the New Chosen People in whom Ben's presumably irreligious father brought him to believe: their teaching preserved in the secular scriptures constituted by *Partisan Review*, *Commentary* and *Encounter*—journals edited, of course, largely by ex-Trotskyite ex-Jews. It is only against this religion of high culture that Ben revolts, as earlier generations had against Judaism, declaring blasphemously at one point, "I hate art"; and at his book's end marching off shamelessly to take a job with Henry Luce, heretic purveyor of mass culture.

But though his father mildly demurs, Ben is not really an oedipal apostate. After all, he has dutifully pursued good grades, published poems, and at one point even done his best to slog his way through René Wellek's *History of Modern Criticism*, a non-Chanukah, non-Christmas present from his father. Moreover, like that father, all his life long, he has lived in communities of ex-Jews like himself. His alienation from the Jewish past, that is to say (it is the novel's penultimate wry joke), has not mitigated his alienation from the gentile present. The enclave of Evanston, Illinois, in which he grows up is as insulated from the gentile Evanston of his neighbors, the true-blue Protestant ladies of the W.C.T.U., as it is from that of the blacks in Chicago just south of its border.

Nor does he really quite "pass" when he goes off to school. At Harvard, where he dreams of fraternizing with the Peabodys, Hearsts, Lodges, and Vanderbilts, he winds up instead in the company of marginal types who "had names," as he rather delicately puts it, "like Weinberg, Feinstein, Cohen. None of them had gone to Groton." So, too, at Oxford, he is snubbed by the proper Anglo-Saxons, both as an American and a Jew; and he seeks consolation in the arms of an imported ex-Jewish girl from the States, who finally runs off with a friend, also an ex-Jew from "home." Ben's alienation, however, is more total than that. Just as he is cut off from the traditional religious culture of gentiles and Jews, he is from the quasi-religious counterculture of his own generation.

Though like many of his age and class he did not, of course, go off to fight in Vietnam side by side with the proles,' black and white, he did not march—either against that war or on behalf of civil rights. When he does wind up in jail at one point, it is not for civil disobedience, but for drunken driving after a quick jump in a sleazy motel.

Even when the political violence in the streets erupts in Chicago, he remains a sightseer, a tourist at someone else's war, really moved only when he spots Allen Ginsberg, Jean Genet, and William Burroughs at the heart of a demonstration. Politics of any sort is for Ben as dead as the Judeo-Christian God. Not only does he tell us nothing about the Trotskyism and Stalinism that moved the writers his father brought him up to venerate; he ignores, too, the rise of the homosexual rights movement and the rebirth of feminism, both of which are occurring before his own eyes. The women in this book are, to be sure, "liberated," but their sexual "freedom" is nonideological, intended only to bug their "liberal," puritan papas.

Consequently, at the book's conclusion Ben is moved to observe, "Somehow the '6os had passed me by . . . whenever I thought back on those years, I invariably saw myself bent monk-ishly over a table in Widener." Yet this is not quite the whole truth either, as Ben goes on to confess, revealing himself as not only more post-Jewish schlemiel than monk, but as a premature yuppie: "I dreamed of a job in New York . . . a nameplate on my desk." Perhaps the fulfillment of that dream lies just beyond the book's conclusion, and with it Ben's final emancipation. As far as the narrative takes us, however, he remains, like his remote ancestors, ghettoized; though to be sure his is a cushy, book-lined ghetto with invisible walls. This constitutes, in any case, the last and best joke in a book that it would be churlish not to admit kept me laughing throughout. But I laughed, as *my* grandmother would have said, *mit yashikes*, with worms, since I was never quite sure who the joke was on—and to tell the truth, I was afraid to find out.

The Many Names of S. Levin
An Essay in Genre Criticism

W H E N I first accepted your invitation to speak here at Oregon State University, I was not sure what aspect of Malamud's work I wanted to talk about, or, indeed, if I wanted to talk about Malamud at all. I have the sense of having said long ago whatever it is I have to say about his books and the generation of Jewish-American writers to which he and I both belong. Frankly the whole subject had begun to bore me a little. But contemplating a return to the Northwest—a trip across the Mississippi, the Great Plains, and finally a passage through the mountains, over the Divide and down the Western Slope, a journey into what had once seemed to me an almost unimaginable future and now has become a nostalgically remembered past—I knew that I must address the subject again after all. And there was only one book I should talk about without betraying my own early adult life and the piety I feel toward it as I enter my sixtieth year. I am referring, of course, to *A New*

Life: the novel in which Malamud evokes and fictionalizes *his* first journey into a West that had begun for him, as for me, as someone else's fiction (goyish images in our Jewish heads) and had to become a part of his own life (a new life for an Easterner, reborn, as all Easterners are reborn in this world) before it could become a part of his fiction.

In the pages of that fiction, by the same token the West itself was reborn as (if you'll pardon the expression) a Jewish West: the American West as a facet of Jewish-American culture, or at least a standard theme of the Jewish-American novel as it had defined itself just after World War II. Though Malamud's book was published in the sixties, it is set in that earlier period. Indeed, it is *about* the fifties almost as much as it is about the West: the age of McCarthyism and the Cold War. I have, therefore, presumed to come to Corvallis to deal with that book, which was conceived here, in total disregard of the ancient adage which warns that in the hangman's house one doesn't mention the rope. But, after all, it was your idea to organize this Malamudian occasion, a clear sign that for most if not all of you a figure once thought of as a pain-in-the-ass or a lovable misfit has been transformed into a cultural monument. And this is a final irony, Corvallis's revenge on Malamud, as *A New Life* was once Malamud's revenge on Corvallis for having failed—as the West always does—his dream, its own dream. But perhaps there is a superirony undercutting the easier ironies with which I have begun, an irony that makes all acts of revenge finally acts of love. It is in that faith, at any rate, that I speak to you today.

Let us properly begin, then, by saying that *A New Life* is a Western, or more accurately a neo- or meta-Western, which is to say, a Western written by an author (typically in a university, where such literature is studied) aware of the tradition, the genre, and therefore a book about that genre as well as about life in the West. It is helpful, I think, to remind ourselves that at the same moment at which Malamud's meta-Western was appearing, another book was being published, very different in every other aspect, but, like *A New Life*, academic in its origins and in its relationship to the tradition of the classic or pop Western. Moreover, like Malamud's novel it, too, is set in the landscape of Oregon, and Oregonians move through its pages. I am thinking of Ken Kesey's *One Flew Over the Cuckoo's Nest*, which, fifteen years after its conception, was detached from the name of its original begetter and re-invented, re-presented by Milos Forman and Jack Nicholson as a Hollywood Western. I have in fact just seen it in that form, in which it has been discovered by an immensely larger audience than ever read it (or even bought it) in print. I hear that a film version of *A New Life* is also being considered; yet I am convinced—for reasons which should be clear to you before I am through—that it will never touch as large and varied a group of viewers as Kesey's book.

The mass audience is able to respond to *One Flew Over the Cuckoo's Nest* at the deepest psychic levels because in the end it proves to be a real Western as well as a meta-Western, or perhaps because it was from the start a real Western merely disguised as a meta-Western. What I intend to suggest (assuming that every genre embodies an archetype, at whose heart is a characteristic myth of love) is that the erotic center of Kesey's novel re-embodies the archetypal Eros underlying the most American of all fictional forms. I have spent a good deal of my life writing about that myth, from my early essay "Come Back to the Raft Ag'in, Huck Honey" to a relatively late study called *The Return of the Vanishing American*, and I like to think there remains scarcely a literate American who is not aware of its structure and meaning. It seems to me, therefore, sufficient at this point to say merely that it is a myth of transitory and idyllic love between two males in the wilderness, one a white refugee from white civilization, the other a nonwhite member of a group that has been exploited or persecuted by his white lover's people. White women, who represent the world of law and order from which the renegade white man is in flight, when they appear in this myth at all appear as the ultimate enemy. Whenever we find such pairs at the center of a fiction, whether they be Twain's Huck and Jim, Cooper's Natty Bumppo and Chingachgook, Melville's Ishmael and Queequeg, Saul Bellow's Henderson and Dahfu, or Kesey's Patrick McMurphy and Chief Bromden, we are in the presence of the true Western.

Never mind the geographical setting. The West is a metaphor for, a mythic name of, the Unexplored wherever it may be: the retreating horizon, the territory that always lies just ahead of where we happen to be, waiting to be penetrated by anyone willing to light out ahead of the rest. Writing just before the cultural revolution that peaked in the late sixties, and prophetically aware of its imminence as Malamud was not, Kesey realized that *inner* space, the new areas of consciousness revealed by experiments with hallucinogenic drugs, represented the unexplored territory for the dying twentieth century better than *outer* space: those lands beyond the Mississippi once identified as the ultimate West. Only a naif like Malamud's S. Levin could still in the fifties take the woods used for experiment by a school of forestry (most of whose graduates would end up behind desks in Washington, D.C.) as the primeval wilderness. But Kesey knew that the logging industry, along with scientific forestry, had long since subdued all American forests; and that a new West would have to be discovered, if the Western were to be preserved as a living mythic form, rather than a subject for irony or sentimentality. The West beyond the ultimate geographical West he located in schizophrenia, which made the madhouse a wilderness beyond the last wilderness, a place in which the Indian comrade would wait still for his refugee white brother, as he was waiting when the first white Europeans set foot on American soil.

Moreover, in Kesey the enemy of that red-white male union and everything it represents is identified, as in all classic Westerns, with the white woman. In older versions of the archetypal form, it was what Mark Twain scornfully called "sivilization" that she advocated against the code of the West with its celebration of flight, violence, and loneliness tempered only by occasional male bonding—in other words, Christian humanism, which is to say, church and school, marriage and the family, and behind them all a sustaining ideal of civil order, social accommodation, and self-control. In Kesey's novel, it is "sanity" and accommodation to a "rational" world that makes heroism impossible, for which the superwhite Big Nurse stands; and he hates her as passionately as he does her program. Malamud, however, is not sufficiently misogynist to write a real Western. Indeed, no one can truly understand or love the West, as it has been mythologized in hundreds of novels and thousands of films and television scripts, who does not hate Respectable White Women, the enforcers of civility and normality—for Kesey the nurse, and for most of his forerunners the schoolmarm.

But S. Levin *is* a schoolmarm, who likes to think of himself as bringing culture and liberal humanism to the barbarian West, meanwhile dreaming of promotion and tenure, making it as a professor, and, who knows, maybe even someday as chairman of a department of English. But this means to imagine a West replete with books and short on guns, a West different from the East only in lower density of population and greater beauty of scenery. He has no vision of the West as an alternative way of life, an altered mode of consciousness, radically different from all we had imported from Europe and reconstructed in the old urban East: the high genteel culture preserved (however inadequately) in the College of the City of New York, as well as in the Ivy League, but disconcertingly undercut by the populist ideals of the land-grant college. Levin ends up, therefore, not by riding off alone, as in the Western movies of my childhood, or dying in the liberating, murderous embrace of his Indian buddy, as in Kesey's book; but by marrying Madame Bovary and heading out for San Francisco (the East in the West, or more precisely imaginary bohemian Europe in ultimate America) to live happily—or unhappily—ever after. It remains a little unclear which; but it doesn't matter, since what happens to him, good or bad, is presented as inevitable, a necessary consequence of what the timid fifties defined as "maturity" or "responsibility."

Malamud's novel is in this sense an anti-Western disguised as a meta-Western, or at least a travesty Western: a tale about failed Westering, the failure of a refugee Easterner to become a Westerner, because he could not abide being reborn in heroic loneliness. Aspiring to become a lover, a husband and a father, he ended up making it only as a fall-back lover, a second husband and a stepfather. What remains obscure in *A New Life*, however, is whether it is the West that fails S. Levin or S. Levin who fails the West, or both. In any case, Malamud's novel is, or at least tries to become, comic; and it belongs, therefore, not, like Kesey's, to the sentimental tradition of Owen Wister, Jack London, and Zane Grey, but to one whose first eminent practitioner was Mark Twain, who also had gone west hopefully, then retreated in amused despair to write a book, get married, and make his fortune. The hero, or rather antihero, of such travesty Westerns is the dude or tenderfoot who can never even learn the language of, much less the ground rules that govern, the strange territory in which he finds himself, whether drawn there by dreams of gold or tenure.

Indeed, as long as *A New Life* remains a burlesque account of a buffoon with a fedora hat on his head, an umbrella in his hand, and a copy of James Joyce's *Ulysses* under his arm, a schlemiel who cannot really believe that the Pacific is really out there over the next range of mountains, and who has never seen a mountain ash or heard of a potluck picnic; a *nebechel* who, in a world where men have gone from horse to automobile to airplane without ever touching the ground, cannot even *drive* (which is to say, is by the definitions of the place impotent), it is not just hilarious, but moving and true. Its fable, moreover, reflects the essential comedy of the West after it has been mythicized by one generation of immigrants and is invaded by the next and the next and the next—being an account of two provincialities meeting head-on in a kind of mutual incomprehension that makes tragedy impossible, since the greatest catastrophe that can eventuate is a pratfall.

And as long as S. Levin remains the absurd antihero on whom kids pee and nervous housewives spill tuna-fish casseroles, I love him and believe in him; as I do, too, when he fails to make it with a barmaid in a barn, or with his aging and anxious officemate on a desk, or when he flees, bare-assed and flustered, sexual defeat piling on sexual defeat. The archetypal eros of the travesty Western is coitus interruptus, the unconsummated act of love. I stay with S. Levin (and with Malamud) even when, en route to a rendezvous with a B−/C+ coed in a motel, he is scared into a ditch by a logging truck and stopped by a mule, which he tries to lure off the road with Life Savers, thereby arriving too late and too undone for anything more fulfilling than a quick (offstage) orgasm and a long troubled sleep. But when Levin finally makes it under the trees with a faculty wife, my credulity grows strained, my interest wanes, and disconcertingly, the West even as a physical setting begins to disappear from the book—along with anything like a genuine confrontation of East and West.

Self-pity, self-righteousness, and a sneaky kind of self-adulation take over from a healthy irony and sense of the ridiculous, as the book slips into what may well be the least rewarding of all American fictional subgenres, the academic novel. In this kind of book, some sensitive representative of the liberal tradition typically finds himself embattled in a world controlled by mindless, callous bureaucrats: deans and department chairmen in academic novel proper, though Big Business or Madison Avenue or Hollywood or the Armed Forces can be substituted for the university without making any essential difference. When he seems at the point of defeat, however, he revenges himself on his persecutors by screwing or running off with the wife of one of them, then retreating to write the very novel the reader holds in his hands. Up until the cop-out point, however, *A New Life* had provided for me, one who has never seduced or decamped with the wife of a dean or a chairman, real vicarious satisfaction. When it appeared, I was close to the end of my own nearly quarter-century-long exile in the West, and it seemed to me at that point that I would never write my own anti-Western.

Yet I felt very much the need for *someone* to get into print an account of the most absurd and touching of all the waves of migration that have ever moved across this country from East to West: the migration of certain upwardly mobile, urban, Eastern young academics, chiefly Jews, into remote, small-town state universities, cow colleges, and schools of education. For various reasons, including a sudden unforeseen growth in enrollment, such institutions were just then rather grudgingly opening their doors to those they would have refused a little while before on ethnic grounds. Yet the moment at which that first Jewish wave of academics reached such alien campuses was the heyday of McCarthyism, when they were most likely to be suspect on political grounds. Indeed, anyone simply urban and Eastern, much less Jewish, was likely in those hysterical times to be suspected of being a troublemaker or a Communist or both, until he had proved otherwise, though he may in fact have left the East with the cry of "red-baiter" or "escapist" ringing in his ears.

All in all, that particular westward migration seems at this point even funnier than the two hilarious ones that followed it: the beatnik march on the Pacific (memorialized without much sense of humor in Jack Kerouac's *On the Road*), and the hippie back-to-the-land movement, whose ebbing has left rusting farm equipment and great patches of cultivated pot everywhere in its wake. It was, to begin with, inadvertent, since most of those involved (including me) did not realize that they were "going West" in any traditional mythic sense. We were just taking what jobs were available in bad times, or simply getting the hell out of a world forever associated for us with the Great Depression, which had exacerbated our normal adolescent angst and impatience with a world we never made. Certainly, we had not the slightest suspicion that in a little while some of us would be hunting and fishing like old-time country-bred WASPs, or wearing string ties and Stetson hats; much less that our consciousness (or failing that, those of the kids we begot in that strange land) might be altered in ways less visible and more profound. But what compounded the comic aspect of the whole adventure even more was that the inadvertent pioneers of the fifties tended to be not just Jews but classic Jewish schlemiels. By a process of negative selection, which I do not quite understand, it was the *nebechel*, the loser, that fled to provincial American campuses from the working class or petty bourgeois communities of Chicago or New York or Brooklyn or Newark, New Jersey. The sharper ones went into business or became doctors, lawyers, or at least wangled their way into more prestigious universities on the Eastern seaboard, or at the very least, in California, which is not what I mean by the West at all.

S. Levin is not untypical in his total schlemielhood, though there can have been few who came like him to an ag school without knowing it, or for that matter, without knowing quite what an ag school was. But he is typical of more than the westward-bound academics of the fifties. Indeed, insofar as *A New Life* records the misadventures of a luckless bumbler, it belongs to a genre with which Jewish writers were concerned long before any of them had heard of Tom Mix or Gary Cooper or John Wayne: a genre with roots in Yiddish folk culture, whose most eminent old-world practitioner was Sholem Aleichem. Moreover, it has influenced the Jewish-American novel, especially in its comic-erotic scenes, ever since the time of Daniel Fuchs and Nathanael West. But this means that insofar as *A New Life* is about the Schlemiel in Love or Out West or In the University, it belongs to the mainstream of Jewish-American fiction.

So why then is S. Levin not a Jew, not really, *really* a Jew, either in his own consciousness, or in that of his colleagues, students, goyish lovers and haters? He seems in this respect less like Malamud's earlier and later protagonists, and more like, say, the leading character in Arthur Miller's *After the Fall*, of whom I once heard a departing theatergoer remark, "If his mother is Jewish and his father is Jewish, how come he ain't Jewish?" We learn quite early in the novel that Levin's father is not just a thief, but a gonif (interestingly, the only other Yiddish word in the book is *luftmensch*), and that he himself used to be a drunkard, for which there is no evidence whatsoever beyond the simple assertion. But perhaps this is an encoded reference to his Jewishness as a stigma he now carefully conceals, even as he tries to live it down. But in another sense, it is surely a denial of that Jewishness, since, as the song I learned on my grandfather's knee has it, "a drunkard is a goy." Or maybe the identification of Levin as an "urban Easterner" is intended to say it all, since that phrase in such a Western small town as Levin inhabits is often a euphemism for "Jew," when not for "Jew-bastard."

Be that as it may, nobody applies the word to him—in rage or anger or simple description—until page 361 of the book's 367 pages. And when it occurs, it is used so obliquely and cagily that nothing could be proved against him in court. "Your picture," Pauline, with whom he is about to run away, says tenderly, "reminded me of a Jewish boy I knew in college who was very kind to me. . . ." There is a hint here, perhaps, of the often embarrassing ritual philo-Semitism common just after World War II among some liberal academics (and particularly among their wives), who were plunged into a crisis of bad conscience after the deaths of the Six Million under Hitler was no longer a secret. Yet our antihero's name, after all, is Levin, S. Levin, Seymour Levin as he calls himself, or Lev as Pauline calls him (only the hostile, indifferent, and insensitive call him "Sy" in an attempt to acclimatize him). A Jewish name in all its changes, one is tempted to say, if there ever was one. But the epigraph from *Ulysses* with which Malamud prefaces his book sends us off on what seems a deliberately planted false scent by equating the name with a perfectly good Old English word meaning "lightning," and directing us to a novel about Dublin written by an Irishman. "Lo, levin leaping lightens/in eyeblink Ireland's westward welkin."

Upon further consideration, however, the Joycean allusion turns out not to be so false a scent after all—suggesting that the ambiguous Jew at the center of this American parable of a stranger in a strange land is derived from a goy's portrait of his own aging, foolish self as an imaginary Jew, or, if you like, a mythological one. And there turn out to be stream-of-consciousness passages attributed to S. Levin in this academic novel that sound like pastiches or parodies of L. Bloom's ruminations on his way from and to home on Eccles Street. Moreover, the word

"westward" in the passage cited provided Malamud, I am convinced, a clue for the geographical translation of Bloom lost in
Ireland to Levin disoriented in the American West. It is a notion
that smacks of the graduate school, but it is as fraught with
pathos and pure comedy as that other classroom inspiration of
Malamud's, to replay T. S. Eliot's version of the Grail legend
in Ebbets Field, which makes for all the best effects (and they
are very good, indeed) in *The Natural*.

If there is another place in the world besides Ireland where
the immemorial conflict of Jew and gentile can be played out
as comedy, burlesque, farce rather than tragedy, it is precisely
the American West. Here, quite as in Ireland, the mythological
hostility of two cultures joined and separated by a common
myth, is not associated with a long history of bloody pogroms
as in Russia or Poland or the Middle East, or with an attempt
at genocide as in Germany. It can therefore be presented in a
tone scarcely more serious than vaudeville skits like Gallagher
and Shean, or hits of the popular comic theater like *Abie's Irish
Rose*. The very notion of the Western Jew is like that of the
Irish Jew a joke in itself. And to understand the sense in which
this is true it is enough, perhaps, just to think of that most
absurd of American aspirants to the presidency, that Jewish
Westerner, or even better, crypto-Jewish Westerner, Barry
Goldwater, or to reflect on the fact that any traditional catch-
phrase out of Western literature becomes hilariously funny the
minute it is spoken with a Yiddish accent: "Smile ven you say
dot, strrengerr!"

In the early chapters of *A New Life*, Malamud seems on the
verge of blending successfully the comic folk traditions of the
schlemiel-schlimazl and the tenderfoot-dude, and combining
both with Joyce's burlesque version of the Wandering Jew as
cuckold, masturbator, and peeper at underdrawers: a culturally
displaced person, who in a world of drinkers cannot drink, only

talk on soberly as everyone else proceeds to get joyously smashed or laid or both. But finally Malamud fails, as his book fails to be funny enough, perhaps out of timidity or pedanticism or squeamishness; or perhaps because (influenced not by what *Ulysses* is, but what it had come to seem in the hands of the academic critics) he wanted to write an art novel, a Great Book, instead of an entertainment or a travesty. At any rate, out of lack of nerve or excess of ambition, he turns S. Levin into a cuckolder rather than a cuckold, a successful lover of women rather than a beater of his own meat, a heroic defender of the liberal tradition, which is to say an insufferable prig like Stephen Dedalus rather than an unloved, lovable victim like Leopold Bloom.

The giveaway, the final offense against the original conception of the book, and its potential for becoming the first real Jewish anti-Western (true ancestor of *Blazing Saddles*) is that there is neither anti-Semitism nor an ironical defense against it to be found in its pages. And how can there be, if there are no Jews, and for that matter, no real goyim either, which is to say, no mythological Westerners? There is not even an ultimately and dangerously appealing shikse, in a deadly sexual encounter with whom ("her invitation wasn't to pleasure, but to struggle, hard and sharp, closer to murder than love . . .") the protagonist of the Jewish-American novel must test his manhood and his Jewishness. Think of the murderous gentile bitches in Ludwig Lewisohn, Ben Hecht, Nathanael West, Philip Roth, Norman Mailer; and then of Pauline in *A New Life*. Poor Pauline, she cannot ever really become the Deadly Stranger Woman, that Faye who always seems Greener on the other side, but has to be satisfied with the role of the Loathly Lady—if big feet and no tits are enough to qualify her for even that mythological role.

After she speaks the magic word "Jewish," however—and it is only she who is permitted to say it—the action promises to turn around, the tone of the book to change from that of condescending satire (the sort of goyish satire endemic to all academic novels), which only puts down the other, to true Jewish irony, which is directed first of all against oneself and one's people, and—at its most intense—against one's God. It is the tone of the Book of Jonah, prototype of all Jewish humor, with its wry comment on the ambiguous meaning of being chosen, i.e., having no choice. When Pauline has finished explaining to Levin that she needed him, wanted him because, however he may have avoided that label, he *looked* Jewish, Levin responds drily, "So I was chosen," and for the first time in many pages I am moved to laugh. But I am puzzled a little as well, since in context the phrase is equivocal; and I am left uncertain about whether in using it Levin is mocking himself for having once been schmuck enough to believe that he *was* chosen as an apostle to the gentiles of Corvallis, Oregon, or whether he is superschmuck enough to believe it still as his story comes to a close.

Immediately thereafter, in any case, he gives himself a new name, or rather reclaims an old one; but this strange rebaptism is even more ambiguous. "God bless you, Lev," the woman he has chosen goes on to say in real or burlesque or merely trivialized benediction. And at that point, he chooses to disavow the name he has allowed her to call him unchallenged throughout, rejecting along with it the cryptic initial S., by which his author has designated him, and "Seymour" as well—that ridiculous pseudoAnglo-Saxon appellation, which like Irving stirs a snigger in polite anti-Semites. Nor does he want any longer to be known as "Sy," an assimilationist nickname, as American as apple pie. "Sam, they used to call me at home," he says; and "God bless you, Sam," she responds in a kind of continuing litany.

The conjunction of "call me" and "Sam"—short, of course,

for Samuel—seems too apt to be unintentional, evoking for me
the image (as if, in typical fashion, Malamud is raising the symbolic ante of his fiction just before he runs out of space) of the
first of the Hebrew prophets, who when God called him by
name answered, "*Hineni*, here I am." *No*, I want to say, don't
do it! It's too pat, too easy, too slick, somehow too *Christian* a
conversion. And then I tell myself, "Come on, Malamud knows
what he's doing. If his hand is on his heart a little melodra-
matically, his tongue is firmly in his cheek, to take the curse
off by undercutting the pretentiousness of the biblical allusion."
But I'm not sure, even though S. Levin does say "Sam" and
not "Samuel," making it possible for us to recall, as we close
the book, not the solemn passage in Kings but the jocularly
anti-Semitic song, "Sam, you made the pants too long." I certainly would prefer to take it this way, for such a reading makes
A New Life in conclusion what it promised to be at the start,
really Jewish and funny as hell.

A Meditation on the Book of Job

ALMOST exactly forty years ago I tried, with all the brash assurance of a neophyte teacher, for the first time to say in public what the Book of Job meant to me. I had been reading and rereading and rereading it ever since I was thirteen or fourteen—in the King James version, of course, in all of whose magnificent inaccuracy I will remember it, I suppose, until the day I die. Certainly I am not prepared to trade the haunting cadences of "Yet man is born unto trouble, as the sparks fly upward" for the more "correct" rendering of the scholarly text before me: "A man is born for trouble / As the sons of Reshef fly upward"—whoever or whatever "Reshef" may be. I could, I know, solve that small mystery by consulting the footnotes. But I am reluctant to do so, having learned over four decades that such information is irrelevant to the solution of larger mysteries at the heart of Job, finally comprehensible, if ever at all, to one not learned but wise—in any case, "full of days."

At some level, I must have been aware of this even when I was very young; but it did not trouble me, because there is much in the text easily available and instantly appealing to readers of that age, consumed with impotent rage against a world that seems a conspiracy against *them*. Obviously, this does not include the speech of resignation with which Job accepts the first series of catastrophes that befall him at Satan's instigation, as he never for a moment suspects—and, as he never for a moment doubts, with the permission of his God. No more was it his initial bland acceptance of the second. Though, or perhaps rather because, I knew the instant clichés with which he responds to both ("The Lord gave, and the Lord hath taken away; blessed be the name of the Lord" and "What? Shall we receive good at the hand of God, and shall we not receive evil?") were especially prized by pious adults, they seemed to me abjectly craven. I did not then suspect—irony being alien to the young—that there might be something ironical, even implicitly subversive in Job's apparent retractions. Nor can I quite make myself believe even now that however attractive such a reading may be to a modern, post–"Death of God" sensibility, it is a true one.

Back then, at any rate, I dismissed the narrative frame-story of Job, the prose Prologue and Epilogue, as a naive anthropomorphic fable beginning with an incomprehensible Wager between God and Satan and ending with a pat, all-too-comprehensible "happily ever after." What I found especially unsatisfactory, however, was Job's unruffled piety in face of the unmerited suffering he endured in between, his infamous "patience." To the self-righteous anger that is the leitmotif of the enclosed verse dialogue, on the other hand, I responded sympathetically. That anger has, to be sure, already erupted even before the Prologue is quite over, when Job ferociously turns on his wife, whom God and the Adversary have, in their to me then still incomprehensible collaboration, strangely spared, as they have not Job's children and his worldly goods. "Curse God and die," she advises him, yielding to the hysteria and despair he has resisted despite all his suffering; and for the first time his equanimity is shattered, so that he screams back at her, "Thou speakest as one of the foolish women speaketh."

At this point, she, anonymous from start to finish, disappears from the book forever, quite as Satan does, after tempting God into the Wager whose final settlement we are not permitted to know, and as Elihu, the fourth "comforter" of Job, will do after speaking his final unanswered condemnation of Job. Before her disappearance into the silence of the text, however, she has triggered the wrath of her husband, suggesting that her response to the monstrous succession of disasters that have befallen him is not just one more calamity, but the last straw. It is a convincing scene, rendered with the utmost economy, though I did not fully understand it until I had lived long enough to learn at firsthand that perhaps the worst effect of seemingly gratuitous household calamity is turning the survivors against each other, as they project the guilt they cannot help feeling for having survived onto those whom they most dearly love, or those who merely happen to be closest at hand. I find it now inevitable, therefore, that what began with the destruction of Job's livestock and servants, then climaxed in the death of his seven sons and three daughters, does not end there. Instead, it descends into the anticlimax of a husband-wife quarrel. But this means, too, that it edges toward, without ever quite slipping over into, burlesque: maintaining an unconsummated flirtation with the comic, which I have come slowly to realize is typical of the comic-tragic work as a whole.

Of all this, however, I was not at first aware; perceiving and relishing not the multiple ironies everywhere present in the Book of Job (the chief of which is his unawareness throughout of what we as readers know from the start, the scandalous Wager in Heaven), but the explicit rage that dominates the dialogue with the Comforters and finally with God himself. Even before he utters his first words to the three Sages who have come from afar, presumably to sustain him in his grief, but who begin a little inauspiciously by mourning for him as if he were already dead, he has exploded: cursing not his Creator, to be sure, but the day he was born, which is to say, the gift of life itself.

Then he cries out with mounting vehemence against the injustice of his own unmerited suffering, and the inherent evil of the entire created world, especially the plight of humankind, doomed, whatever good or ill may befall them in their brief span of existence, to die forever. His most venomous invective, however, he reserves for his pious Comforters, who, finding his insistence on blaming not himself but God for his plight blasphemous, respond in kind.

Eliphaz, to be sure, who answers him first, begins by trying—or at least pretending—to speak sympathetically. But his patience soon runs out, as Job maintains his "integrity" and insists on his right to quarrel with his Maker; and he ends by railing against Job as vituperatively as his companions, Bildad and Zophar, who are enraged from the start by Job's "unorthodox" contention (with which, to be sure, God has in the Prologue agreed) that humankind and he in particular sometimes suffer "for nothing."

They grow even more furious as Job's anger, mounting in response to their own, is directed at the sanctimonious platitudes with which they, immune to pain, try to explain away the injustice he is experiencing in his own rotting and pain-ridden flesh. His suffering, they explain, is, like all human suffering, a punishment for sin, a discipline that purifies the soul: to deny this, they go on, is to compound sin, but to confess it and repent will bring in the end recompense and reward. They do not, however, speak reassuringly but in reproach and exasperation.

Finally, what was begun as a theological argument in verse becomes a screaming match. Never has poetry been made at a higher decibel level or a steeper pitch of acrimony, which is further raised when a fifth participant in the debate appears out of nowhere, his intervention unmotivated and unprepared for. He is, we are almost immediately informed, younger than Eliphaz, Bildad, or Zophar, and presumably Job as well. Certainly, he is—as perhaps befits his age—angrier than the rest, his anger directed not just against Job, who has still not ceased to argue his case, but against the other three, who have stopped contending with him. Even before we learn what he is called, we learn of his anger: the introductory tag in the text reads, "Then was kindled the wrath of Elihu, the son of Barachel the Buzite against Job . . . because he justified himself rather than God. And against his three friends . . . because they found no answer. . . ."

He is an oddly shadowy figure, this Elihu, despite the fact that (ironically once more) he is called by a Jewish name, the name in fact of the great prophet of Israel. He represents, I am convinced, an afterthought, a last desperate attempt on the part of the poet who gave the Book of Job its final form, to defend orthodoxy against Job's subversive challenge, which that poet, like Elihu, apparently believed had not yet been satisfactorily confuted.

Yet though he has seemed problematically present to all readers and commentators ever since, that metatextual kibbitzer is invisible and inaudible to the rest of the dramatis personae, who neither respond to him nor acknowledge his presence. Even Job, whom Elihu, unlike the three other Sages, calls by name over and over in an almost comically vain attempt to attract his attention, ignores him. Moreover, so also does the Lord, whose thunderous Voice out of the Whirlwind drowns out the last echoes of Elihu's peroration, as if to make clear that it is to Him the final word belongs, rather than to that presumptuous upstart who has tried to preempt His privilege.

He does not even in His all-encompassing righteous wrath (for Him, too, anger seems the chief motive for discourse) deign to condemn Elihu, as He does Eliphaz and his fellows for "not having spoken of him the thing which is right." Nor does He address him in an attempt to bully him into silence, as He does Job, who, He indicates, indirectly and backhandedly, has spoken of Him truly. But what this means remains unclear. Does it amount to a confession—extorted from Him who will not even reveal the scandalous Wager that began everything—that He is, indeed, as Job contends and his Comforters deny, one who "destroyeth the perfect and the wicked" and "will laugh at the dismay of the innocent"? But He does not finally destroy Job, whom He has described as perfect, nor laugh at his plight; he restores him at the poem's end to health and prosperity.

We are confronted again with an apparent contradiction between what is said in the enclosed poetic Dialogue and what we are told in the framing prose story. In the latter, God proves finally to be a God of Mercy, who "blessed the latter end of Job more than the beginning." But in the theophany that concludes the former, he manifests himself as a God of Wrath, the creator of all in the natural world that is hostile to and unconquerable by man: Behemoth, the phallic monster, the nerves of whose testicles are intertwined and whose penis is like the lofty cedar; and the Leviathan, that fiery engine of destruction who makes the very deeps boil like a pot. At this point Job declares, "I have heard of thee by the hearing of my ear; but now mine eye seeth thee . . ."; suggesting he has learned at last what his long suffering had not taught him: not merely that God is beyond good and evil, but that He reveals Himself only to one willing to maintain this unpalatable truth over the objections of the pious.

At age fourteen, at any rate, I identified myself with Job thus understood, though, alas, unlike him, I did not believe, or at least I *believed* I did not believe, in God. I had, therefore, no one to blame for my own misery and the palpable injustice of the world around me (it was the time of the Great Depression) except for "society," "history," "heredity," and "environment"—dumb abstractions incapable of answering anything. Nonetheless, I persisted in speaking what I hoped were Jobean truths that the pious of our own time, my parents and teachers, considered blasphemous; and dreaming in spite of all that a Voice from Somewhere would somehow declare that I had spoken the thing which was right.

By the time I reached the age of thirty, however, I had come to believe I believed in Job's God—just in time to blame Him for the near annihilation of European Jewry, through which, to be sure, I had lived at a safe distance, but in which every member of my family still in the Old World died. So also I cried out against Him for the horrors of World War II, which I had experienced at firsthand, having survived the Battle of Iwo Jima, and (the final horror perhaps) having rejoiced when, as a Japanese interpreter assigned to monitoring Radio Tokyo, I heard the news of the dropping of the bomb on Hiroshima. But of this I was not ashamed then and am not now, since it meant the end of the mutual slaughter I could no longer abide. Of the role that human error and villainy, including my own, played in these events, I was aware; but they seemed too petty to explain away disasters so cosmic in scope. Such suffering "for nothing" only a God of the Cosmos, omniscient, omnipotent, but vindictive or indifferent, a Hangman God, could have, *must* have—for reasons unknowable and unthinkable to mere humans—instigated or, in any case, permitted.

Consequently, I took the first opportunity afforded me to cry out against Him, like Job, challenge Him to justify Himself. As if I were some unconvincing counterfeit of the role I sought to play, however, an Elihu pretending to be Job, He did not answer me—not out of the Whirlwind, nor even inside the silence of my troubled head. Yet what could I have expected? When I was at last able to speak out on Job's behalf in public, I was no lonely sufferer on a metaphoric ash-heap, but a Ph.D. hired by the state to lecture to freshmen at the University of Montana.

It was, to be sure, a setting no more remote and improbable than the Land of Uz, another Edom in fact. Moreover, the spiritual descendants of Job's scandalized Comforters had gathered together to confront me. Indeed, as soon as the word went out that I, a Jew from the urban East (which is to say, a "communist" and "atheist" until proved otherwise), was going to expound the Scriptures to good Christian children, fundamentalist preachers came from far and near to monitor what I said.

To make matters worse, the course in which I was lecturing was called Introduction to the Humanities, suggesting to them that what I was about to teach was "humanism," "secular humanism": dread words even then to those who had not yet begun to speak of themselves as the "moral majority." That I considered myself not a skeptical secularist but a Hebrew of the Hebrews, an apostle to the gentiles, mattered to them not at all. In any case, I was the enemy, to be watched as warily as I in turn watched them, sitting side by side at the very back of the auditorium, where they scribbled notes on my "blasphemies" that they then duly transmitted to the chairman of my department and the president of the University.

What offended them from the start, confirming their worst suspicions, was my insistence that my Job, *our* Job was not "patient" at all, though in *their* tradition he had become a proverbial example of that presumably Christian virtue. In the main body of the Dialogue, I contended, he refused to submit in silence to the will of God, but instead impatiently challenged Him in ever increasing rage. But, I assured my listeners, this ongoing quarrel with their Maker whenever he seemed to infringe the Law he had given to his People is an essentially Jewish tradition. So the prophets and the psalmist cry out in indignation because the race is not to the swift and the contest to the strong, and ask angrily why the wicked prosper. So, too, we are told, Abraham risked divine wrath by protesting against the destruction of Sodom, and Jonah sulked and grumbled at the last-minute salvation of Nineveh.

Equally "Jewish," I further argued (not troubling to make clear that this was only true in pre-Rabbinical times), is Job's rejection of the doctrines of the resurrection of the body and the immortality of the soul, his insistence that when we die, as we all must, we die forever, and that therefore justice must be done us, if God is just, here and now. Or perhaps, I went on to speculate, what the redactors of the Old Testament and especially the author of Job meant to suggest is that we must act *as if* there were no life after death, so that our righteous demand for justice in this world not be undercut by the (perhaps delusive) hope that in the next the wicked will be punished and the virtuous be rewarded. In any case, I concluded, even more offensively, I guess, that Job could in no sense be considered, as the Fathers of their faith had argued, a prototype of Jesus, who had gone without a mumbling word of protest to the sacrificial death decreed for him by his "Father in Heaven."

Paradoxically enough, however, I reminded the goyim before me, Job had been a goy like them, apparently quite unaware of God's Covenant with Abraham or the Giving of the Law to Moses on Mount Sinai. Certainly neither he nor his Comforters, whose very names, except for that of Elihu, indicate that they are Idumeneans, Edomites, betray any knowledge of the special laws and rituals that separate YHVH's Chosen People from the gentiles. Even in his "negative confession" in Chapter 31, Job declares himself guiltless only of those "sins" forbidden in the Noachite Code, injunctions, the rabbis believed, known to all men without special revelation. Moreover, throughout the poetic center of the book, the four-letter Hebrew cult name for the Lord is avoided in favor of nonspecific designations like Shaddai, El, Eloah, and Elohim.

Jesus, on the other hand, was, as Job presumably was *not*, circumcised on the eighth day; and though finally found heretical by the High Priest, he seems always to have thought of himself as a Jew, promising his followers that not one *yod* or tittle of the Law would pass away. Nonetheless, in the Prologue God Himself, called at one point YHVH, disconcertingly describes Job as "perfect," and in the Epilogue, again in that name, declares the rightness of all he has said. Yet despite this, both orthodox Jews and Christians have accepted the Book of Job as canonical. But why, I asked, *why?*—and none of the watchdog clerics answered. Indeed, none of them ever rose to challenge me face to face, unwilling to reenact their archetypal roles in the mythological script I felt myself to be reenacting.

Maybe it was because they felt embarrassed by my show of scholarship. During the years between the War's ending and my return to teaching, I had (fumbling tentatively back toward the faith of my ancestors) studied Hebrew at the Harvard Divinity School. There I had learned enough of the Holy Tongue to plod through the simple prose of the frame story of Job, and in a class called Exegesis of the Prophets, taught by Robert

Pfeiffer, I had acquired some of the jargon and simpler techniques of the "higher criticism"—enough apparently to cow into silence the fundamentalist clergy of Missoula, Montana. Or perhaps they were only bored when I began, more than a little pretentiously, I fear, to throw about words like "hapalogomena" and "theodicy." In any case, as I abandoned the open language of myth for the hermetic abstractions of the academy, they drifted away one by one.

Finally, I was left alone with my students, who of course did not argue back either. They were too busy taking notes in preparation for the upcoming midterm examination to really listen as I attempted to "justify God's ways to man," or rather to present what I took to be the Job poet's attempt. For the atheist, I explained, the presence of gratuitous human suffering in a world produced by blind chance and mindless evolution is no problem at all. Nor did it seem one to the ancient Greeks, who thought of men as the playthings of amoral immortals, often at odds with each other, and always at the mercy of fate. Still less were the Manichees troubled, since they believed the universe to be ruled by two eternally contending principles of light and dark. As for the Hindus, I went on remorselessly, they were able—believing as they did in reincarnation—to explain the suffering of any individual, however blameless, in terms of "bad karma" inherited from moral failures in an earlier existence. A similar way out was available to orthodox Christians, who had somehow managed to derive from the myth of the Temptation in the Garden the doctrine of Original Sin: the notion that "in Adam's Fall we sinned all," and that therefore we all of us, guilty from birth, deserve whatever calamities befall us. Unless, to be sure, by believing in Jesus as the Christ, we are saved. That even such true believers (indeed Christ himself) are sometimes martyred for that belief, the Fathers of the Church could scarcely deny. But there was always the fallback doctrine that amends would be made after death, transient earthly suffering rewarded with eternal heavenly bliss.

But this cop-out of "pie in the sky," I insisted (trying to use the dialect of my auditors, as I noticed some of them beginning to nod and doze), was scorned by the author of Job, who was convinced that "as the cloud is consumed and vanisheth away; so he that goeth down to the grave shall come up no more." Consequently, his protagonist demands of his God—whom, enlightened pagan that he is, he believes to be One, omniscient, omnipotent, and above all just—justice *here and now*. It never occurs to him, moreover, that evil might be, as later philosophers argued, the mere absence of good, much less illusory, unreal. One can imagine the incredulity with which he would have greeted Socrates' assertion that in some sense, the highest sense perhaps, "No harm can befall a good man, living or dead." Job knows he is a good man and that the suffering inflicted on him is temporally and sub specie aeternitatis real; and he asks, hoping for no other recompense, to be told *why*.

He therefore requires of his God, whom he desperately hopes is *answerable*, the answer that mere men cannot give, certainly not the Sages who seek to alleviate his discomfiture with bland platitudes to which that very discomfiture gives the lie. Nor will he be silenced when that God—improbably, unexpectedly—appears to him, speaking out of the whirlwind. We seem to tremble for a moment on the verge of his desired Happy Ending, the resolution of the problem of unmerited suffering. But (in another typically ironic turn of the screw) what the answerable God answers, in wrath and exasperation, is that there is no answer—at least none understandable to a mere human, who does not even understand the monstrous in the created world. Yet this anticlimactic non-answer Job seems to find satisfactory, subsiding, at any rate, into silence more like one who is truly satisfied, rather than merely cowed or subdued, as I believed when I was very young.

Certainly this is the meaning of Job's final explanation for his capitulation, "I have read of thee by the hearing of the ear; but now my eye seeth thee;/ Wherefore I abhor myself and repent in dust and ashes." Understanding these verses, we understand that Job was given not less but more than he had asked for, more than he had known how to ask for. He sought only to be enlightened in his own grieving heart and to be justified in the sight of his fellows, to understand and to be understood. He was granted instead a moment of mystical transport, a glimpse of the Divine Essence. In that dazzling moment, it is suggested that precisely for this reason the righteous are chosen for egregious and gratuitous suffering, which alone can deliver them from the pious lies with which the orthodox seek to euphemize the Mystery of Evil and God's terror at its heart—thus enabling them to see Him face to face.

This, back then in Missoula, I took to be the final solution to the problem of the theodicy offered by the Book of Job. In fact, even now, as I approach three score and ten, I consider it still crucial to an understanding of that enigmatic work. I have come to realize, however, that it is a partial reading only, which by concentrating on the framed poetic dialogue ignores the two framing Mysteries of Prologue and Epilogue that qualify such a solution: the Mystery of the Wager and the Mystery of Restoration. It seems to me now, indeed, that the Dialogue, though (or because) its participants are portrayed as ignorant of the Wager throughout, represents an attempt to translate the Mystery it embodies in haggadic form into abstract terms more congenial to its latter-day theologian-poet. But like all such attempts at translating multivalent mythos into univocal logos, this attempt turns out to be not merely reductive but sufficient only unto its own day. Later abstract thinkers have, therefore, felt compelled to retranslate it again and again into the theological or scholarly jargons fashionable in their own time.

God knows there have been many of them, Jewish, Christian, humanist, positivist, existentialist: ranging from Moses Maimonides to Martin Buber, Gregory the Great and Calvin to Kierkegaard and Reinhold Niebuhr, Thomas Hobbes and Immanuel Kant to Josiah Royce and Paul Weiss. However dialectically subtle, their interpretations, twice removed, reductions of reductions, are lacking in archetypal resonance. Whatever light they cast on their own authors and their era, I find them consequently not very helpful in coming to terms with the work they pretend to explicate, much less to the triune Mystery at its core. Still less helpful are the scholarly commentaries, recent and contemporary, through which I have felt compelled to slog my weary way in preparation for writing this, my last word on Job. Though they solve certain lexical and textual problems in the Dialogue, suggesting meanings for rare and difficult words, and reordering rationally such obviously garbled and lacuna-ridden passages as Chapters 24 to 27, they do little to illuminate the tantalizingly ambiguous Frame. Nor should they, since its ambiguity is not accidental but essential.

More useful in this regard—since they preserve that ambiguity—are the more properly haggadic interpolations into and extensions of the ancient folktale, of which there are also, thank God, numerous examples. As is characteristic of all truly archetypal narrative, the core Job fable has survived, for simpler readers at least, outside the interpretive contexts in which the redactor of the Book of Job and his successors have tried to enclose it. Indeed, it has, as it were, insisted on being told and retold *as a story*, ever growing and changing—or rather, seeking to complete itself, to find its entelechy, its final form. Such accretions and transformations began as early as The Testament of Job, and the not-very-faithful "translation" of the Septuagint;

continuing in Muslim holy texts, the rabbinical midrashim, and the interpretive parables of the Zohar. Closer to our own time, the body of Judaic legend spawned by the archetypal substrate of Job has been gathered together for readers of English by Louis Ginzberg, and richly reimagined in *Messengers of God*, that midrash of midrashim, composed by the Nobel laureate Elie Wiesel as he meditated on the Holocaust.

Nor has it been absent from the secular literature of the goyish West. Both its form (he considered it the prototype for the Brief Epic or Epyllion) and its content profoundly influenced John Milton's *Paradise Regained*; and Goethe palpably adapted its mythos in the "Prologue in Heaven" of *Faust*. In our own century, it has been retold in an updated version in H. G. Wells's novel, *The Undying Fire*; and Robert Frost has recast it, with oddly feminist overtones, in his poem, "A Masque of Reason." It was, moreover, turned into a strange little playlet by Thornton Wilder, called "Hast thou considered my servant, Job"; and in 1955, Archibald MacLeish's verse drama, *J. B.*, starring Christopher Plummer and Raymond Massey and directed by Elia Kazan, became a smash hit on Broadway.

In the process, the Book of Job itself has come to be regarded by many not as "scripture" but as "poetry"—in the words of Tennyson, "the greatest poem of ancient and modern times"; which is to say, no longer a work to be read as a guide to wisdom and salvation but as one to be preserved in libraries and taught in classes in "literature." Rereading it, therefore, we find it harder and harder these days to hear in our inner ear the storyteller's voice, spinning a tale never heard for the first time or the last, always different though always the same: "There was a man in the land of Uz whose name was Job . . ." Yet even the most secular versions send us back, at last, from the analytic Dialogue to the oneiric Frame, which signifies as dreams do: its images, overdetermined, polysemous, finally inexhaustible.

Most useful in this regard are the midrashim, for whose inventors "literature" had not yet been separated from "scripture."

Primarily through them, in any case, I have been led back to the Prologue and Epilogue I had so long ignored; though, to be sure, much that troubled the rabbis who created them does not much interest me. Some of them sought, for instance, in their addenda to resolve ambiguities in the original fable about whether Job was a Jew or a gentile, and whether in either case he was circumcised—born without a foreskin, perhaps, as befits one called *tam*. Others tried to make clear his marital status, some insisting that he had had one wife, some two, and in either case naming those spouses. I am, however, convinced that he was an uncircumcised goy and remain indifferent to whether he begot his second family on the woman who bore his first or on someone else. Yet I must confess that I am a little intrigued by the notion that after the death of his first wife he married Dinah, the daughter of Jacob, who was terribly raped and revenged, so that quite properly, if rather ironically, he could on his deathbed warn the children she bore him against intermarrying with gentiles. I could not care less, moreover, whether after his death he, who denied the immortality of the soul, was granted a share in the life to come, as some rabbis insisted he was not.

What chiefly interests me are the attempts of the rabbis to suggest, by filling in lacunae in the original tale, reasons why blameless Job of all men had been chosen by the Adversary to suffer, and especially why God had assented. In several often repeated midrashim, he is portrayed as having been before the time of his testing a counselor to the Pharaoh of the Exodus story. Consulted, along with those other gentile prophets, Balaam and Jethro, as to whether the midwives of Egypt should be ordered to kill the newborn sons of the Jews, he refused to answer or equivocate. Therefore, unlike Balaam, who strongly urged their slaying, and is damned, or Jethro, who argued against it and is blessed (becoming, indeed, grandfather to the children of Moses), Job is destined to endure both good and evil, turn and turn about. Other traditional Jewish tales, however, portray Job not as a moral equivocator, but a guiltless gentile scapegoat whom God offers to Satan to keep him from inflicting harm on less innocent Jews. So for instance, we are told, God used him to save Abraham, whom the Adversary had rightly accused of infringing the Law by substituting one sacrifice for another on the altar; or else to preserve from drowning the Children of Israel, whom at the moment of their crossing the Red Sea the Enemy of Mankind charged (once more justly) with having bowed down to strange gods in Mizraim.

Other midrashim sought to explain not so much God's apparent complicity in Job's unmerited tribulations, as Satan's having chosen him in the first place. Job had, such stories inform us, in his time of prosperity desecrated a shrine set up in Satan's honor, thus demonstrating (at least so the Zohar interprets it) an unwillingness to pay proper respect to "the Other Side," which, the writers of that mystic book insist, the Torah itself enjoins. What else does the Holy Text mean, they argue, by urging us to worship "with all our hearts," except that we must serve Him also with the *yetzer-ha-ra*, the Evil Impulse—another name for Satan, they further teach—as well as the Good.

Nor is their subtle and disturbing charge against Job without foundation. Neither in the fabulous frame story nor in the enclosed poetic theodicy of the Book of Job does its protagonist ever allude to Satan by any of his names, as if he were not merely unwilling to give the devil his due, but could not even conceive of his existence. When his multiple calamities befall him, Job attributes them not to the natural catastrophes or human enemies, whom the narrative tells us are their proximate cause; but still less does he fix responsibility for them on a supernatural Adversary. For him God is the sole author of all that befalls humankind, evil as well as good.

Nor does anything in the text call this assumption into question. Indeed, God Himself in his final appearance seems to verify it, confessing nothing about the Wager in Heaven and saying nothing to imply the existence of its instigator. But why? Is He who speaks out of the Whirlwind (as a few embittered modern commentators have dared to suggest) ashamed to admit to the frail human being who has successfully passed His terrible test that He Himself has failed an earlier one? Or is He thus revealed as a hoaxster, a cheat, in this black comedy's last and blackest joke? Before answering, we should pause long enough to note that the narrator, too, is silent at this point about Satan, who does not even appear—as we might well expect, approaching the tale's Happy Ending—to be discomfited and cast out.

It is as if (or so I read it, paying attention to its silences as well as its statements) what the encrypted text suggests is that Satan does not finally exist except as a metaphor for what can be understood once God is fully revealed as an aspect, a projection, an emotion of the One who alone really is forever. All the more is this true of those surrogates for Satan, Job's wife and the egregious Elihu, who at this point also disappear from the book, having been, like the *yetzer-ha-ra* itself, assumed into the Divine Unity. But at this YHVH has already hinted in his parabolic speech about the Behemoth and the Leviathan. "These things of Darkness," he has declared in effect, "I acknowledge mine."

Surely here is the final clue to the meaning of the Mystery of the Wager with the Adversary, to whom we were first introduced standing at ease with his fellow *b'nai Elohim* before the Heavenly Throne. It is with Himself that God is betting: with His own "Other Side," from which He cannot otherwise exorcize the suspicion that no man, not even Job, His "perfect" servant, does good "for nothing." It is this nagging doubt that entices Him into making the cruel test, whose outcome, we tell ourselves, He surely knows from the start. But then, like Him perhaps, we remember how Adam, similarly tempted, fell. Certainly, ever since that mythological event, which is to say, since mankind first knew Good from Evil, we have been haunted by doubts about our own virtue, which we project in fear and trembling upon our Maker.

After all, Job is a work written by man and not God, as even the rabbis taught, attributing its composition to Moses, but insisting that unlike the Pentateuch it was not the product of divine inspiration. Moreover, one or two of them also insisted, it was to be read as a *masal*—a myth or parable rather than history; and read so, it seems to me a revelation, psychological rather than theological, that we *want* to be thus tempted by God, *want* the doubt about ourselves, which we attribute to Him, to be resolved in our favor. Only after this, in the wish-dream that constitutes the true heart of Job, comes the long-awaited Happy Ending. At this point, however, we pass from the Mystery of Evil to the even greater Mystery of Restoration, which, I must confess, I have as yet barely begun to understand. I suspect, indeed, that I never shall, unless like Job (but God forbid that I pay the price) I am granted a double three score years and ten in addition to those I have already lived. Until then, therefore, I am moved like him "to lay my hand upon my mouth," and to repeat his penultimate vow of silence, which finally, to be sure, he did not keep: "Once have I spoken . . . yea, twice; but I will proceed no further."

In Every Generation
A Meditation on the Two Holocausts

F OR a long time now I have resisted all importunities
to confront head-on in print the destruction by Hitler of six
million Jews, what has come to be called the "Holocaust."
It is in part this intrinsically theological name for an essentially
secular atrocity that has put me off. Not merely has it become
an instant cliché, but by employing it (as how can I not?) I
predetermine, as it were, my own attitudes and the response
of my audience. Think how different those attitudes and that
response would be if I were to use more neutral sociological
terms like "genocide"; or even the Nazis' mythological one, the
"Final Solution."

Moreover, I have always been afraid that in dealing with that
subject I could not keep from seeming to suggest that I, who
as an American was safely removed from the European catastrophe, have been, insofar as I am at least allegedly Jewish, in
some sense its victim. It is true, of course, that Hitler would

have considered me a Jew (whatever my own doubts about my identity); but this gives me, I am convinced, no right to exploit—rhetorically, politically, philosophically—the ultimate misery of those alien others with whom he would have lumped me. At any rate, both my Jewishness and theirs remain for me even now not a given fact but an enigma, elevated by their fate as victims and mine as an unscathed survivor (perhaps to some degree a victimizer) if not quite to the level of a full theological Mystery, at least to that of a modest lower-case "mystery." It is, in any event, this minor mystery that I propose to explore in the subtheological meditation that follows: a meditation on not just one Holocaust, but—for reasons I hope will become clear before I am through—two.

Unlike many religious thinkers (though I speak their language, it should be understood that what for them is revealed truth is for me myth and metaphor), I do not consider the failed total destruction of European Jewry a *novum*—an event not merely monstrous but unprecedented, unique, and, therefore, incomprehensible, ineffable. It seems to me in retrospect disconcertingly predictable: an occurrence, or better, perhaps, a reoccurrence in history of what already existed out of historical time; which is to say, an event that had long since become a myth, the key myth, indeed, of Jewish existence.

My maternal grandfather, who had before he was quite full grown fled the Eastern European world of pogroms and the threat of pogroms, when asked what was happening in the world, would usually answer (at least so I remember it), "Nothing new. *M'hargert yidd'n*. They're killing Jews. What else?" The first time I heard it, I was left wondering whether it was some strange kind of adult joke at which, if I lived so long, I would be able someday to laugh. But it no longer seemed a joke of any kind, when at age seven or eight I found myself reenacting in fact that myth of our history. I was then a student in a suburban New Jersey grade school, where my brother and I constituted half of the total Jewish enrollment. We felt ourselves, therefore, interlopers in a goyish institution, where, of course, all of our teachers were goyim and we had weekly school "chapels," at which we were expected to repeat *their* "Lord's Prayer" and, at the appropriate seasons, sing hymns celebrating the birth and resurrection of *their* Christ.

All of this, however, had made me only a little uncomfortable, until one day in the schoolyard all hell broke loose. During recess and after class, when my fellow students gathered together to choose up sides for a game, more often than not they would end with Protestants on one side and Catholics on the other (for me it was a baffling distinction without a difference), then proceed to pummel each other in a kind of mock Holy War. On this occasion, however, for reasons I still don't understand, they noticed me slinking off alone, as I customarily did; and remembering that I was a Jew, which is to say, the legendary enemy of both, joined together to chase me all the way home, screaming, "You killed our Christ."

At that moment of sheer funk (I was sure that they meant really, *really* to kill me), I learned not only that my grandfather's joke was not a joke at all, but the reason why Christians had long slaughtered us in earnest: their myth of the Jews. But, of course, I did not yet know how to say this even to myself, much less my pursuers. If I had been able to find breath for anything but running I would probably have shouted, "What, I killed your Christ? I wasn't even there." Certainly, I would not have had the chutzpah, even if I had the breath, to answer their charge of deicide with the defiant affirmation I was to hear years later on the streets of Jerusalem. It was in the midst of the turbulent sixties, when a band of irreverent young Israelis cried aloud to watching tourists, including me, "We did so kill him. We did so!"

But after all, those marchers were at home in a world of their fellows, while I (as I realized first back then in New Jersey) was a stranger in a strange land, and would remain so to the day of my death. No matter that I could already read the language of the land to which my forebears had fled, better, speak it better, write it better than my child persecutors, to whose ancestors it "belonged" as it did not to mine. As a matter of fact, this only made matters worse.

Perhaps it would have helped if I had been familiar with the Jewish countermyths explaining the hostility between us and the gentiles, myths invented before Jesus had claimed to be the Messiah, and had been condemned by the High Priest of Israel as a blasphemer, then turned over to the dubious justice of Rome. The key text is, of course, the passage in the Haggadah for Pesach, repeated annually by all who consider themselves still Jews: "for not one only hath risen up against us, but in every generation there are some who rise up against us: but the Most Holy, blessed be he, hath delivered us out of their hands." "In every generation," the threat warns us, looking forward to Hitler and Muslim terror as well as backward to Haman and the Pharaoh, "who knew not Joseph."

But it is not the final word, being followed by a promise of deliverance, which reminds us that not merely did six million Jews die in the "Holocaust," but more millions escaped alive to tell the tale. It is, indeed, their survival and subsequent fate that is for me the true, the final mystery. Before returning to it, however, I feel obliged to wrestle with the question of *why* the threat of annihilation and the promise of redemption have continued to be the pattern of our history. Here, too, there is a traditional text suggesting an answer: the cryptic Chapter 53 of Isaiah, in which the prophet imagines the kings of the gentiles confessing that only through the suffering they inflict on God's faithful servant, Israel, can they themselves be saved: "Surely he hath born our griefs, and carried our sorrows: yet we did esteem him stricken, smitten of God and afflicted./But he was wounded for our transgression, he was chastised for our iniquities; the chastisement of our peace was upon him: and with his stripes we are healed."

It was not, however, until I was approaching middle age that I became aware of those texts and their relevance to my own fate as well as that of my people; which is to say, not until after the defeat of Hitler, the revelation of the full horror of the concentration camps and the simultaneous loss of my earlier faith in socialism and the universal brotherhood of all mankind. I was a communist of the Stalinist persuasion at age thirteen, a Trotskyite before I was twenty. My holy books, therefore, were not the Torah and Talmud, but the collected works of Marx, Engels, and Lenin, which seemed to me then to teach the True Way: not just a way to make a better world but a way to escape the limitations of my ancestral religion. To be sure, those limitations were not very onerous, since neither my parents nor my grandparents observed the rules of kashruth, nor were they members of any congregation. But they had nonetheless preserved intact in the New World the parochialism and xenophobia that had been concomitants of Old World Judaism.

Though my grandfather no longer recited the morning blessings in which he thanked his Creator for not having made him a goy, when I behaved intelligently, he praised my *yiddisher kopf*, and when I acted stupidly, he reproached me for having a goyish one. For my grandmother, who kept none of her opinions secret, all gentiles were contemptible: the Irish, the Italians, and especially those from whose midst she had fled, the Poles, along with the *schwarzers*, the Negroes, who seemed to her their American equivalents. Even in the mouths of my native-born parents, the words *shegetz* and shikse were epithets of contempt, and I was not surprised to discover that the root meaning of these standard words for a gentile male and female is "abomination." Small wonder, then, that the parents of my favorite high school teacher, a Jew, sat *shiva* for him when he married a shikse, mourned for him as if he were dead.

To be sure, I was aware that such Jewish hatred and fear of their non-Jewish neighbors was reflexive, a reaction to generations of persecution in Eastern Europe—and that, of course, it was finally impotent as well, drawing not a single drop of gentile blood in return for the buckets of Jewish blood shed by the gentiles for so many generations. Yet it was, I knew, weakness rather than charity that had made my people in their long exile settle for calling upon their God to pour out his wrath on the goyim, instead of slaughtering them themselves as their ancestors had done, when moving into the Promised Land.

In any event, I was convinced in those days that until such mutual recrimination and hostility ceased, until anti-Semitism and anti-anti-Semitism alike were ended, there could be no social peace. Nor would it cease, I believed, until the International Soviet had become the human race, until in a world without poverty, exploitation, and greed there were no longer Christians and Muslims, Hindus and Buddhists—and, yes, no longer Jews. Though I did not then go on record, in the thirties my response to a question about the future of American Jewry would doubtless have been much like that of Henry Roth, who wrote three decades later: "I feel that to the great boons Jews have already conferred upon humanity, Jews in America might add this last and greatest one: of orienting themselves toward ceasing to be Jews."

Since one of the boons of the Jews to humanity to which Roth was referring was clearly Marxism, I felt that in abandoning Judaism in favor of socialism I was merely swapping an earlier, lesser Jewish faith for a later, greater one. After all, I assured myself, Marx had been ethnically Jewish; and from the start his doctrines had been especially appealing to his fellow Jews. Of this I became aware early on when my grandfather, wanting to teach me a little Yiddish, began by making me sound out in the *mammeloshen* the masthead slogan of the *Daily Forward*: "Workers of the World Unite!" My father, to be sure, was a violent anti-Marxist; but being as confirmed an atheist as he was an American patriot (he dreamed that I or my brother would make it into West Point), he brought me up reading Bob Ingersoll and Tom Paine, to whom organized religion was also anathema.

The mythological Hebrew texts to which I alluded at the beginning of this meditation were therefore quite unknown to me until I was closing in on middle age and had become the father of three sons. It was at that point that, finding myself and them all the more strangers in a strange land in Missoula, Montana, I organized the first seder I had ever attended: a communal celebration for a handful of fellow Jewish exiles, most of them also teachers in the State University and, predictably enough, almost none of them married to Jewish women. It was in that congregation, at any rate, that I first heard ringing in my ears (in my own voice and, of course, in English) the warning that "in every generation there are some who rise up against us" and began to puzzle out its meanings.

Even earlier I had begun to wrestle with the second key text, when, just after the end of World War II, I spent a full semester in the Harvard Divinity School, studying the twelve mysterious verses that constitute that fifty-third chapter of Isaiah. I had gone there to learn Hebrew, but why I was not really sure. I was motivated perhaps by a desire to rediscover—or, more accurately, to invent for the first time—my Jewishness, though there was a certain irony in my attempting to do so in a Christian school, as there was also in my simultaneously joining a choral group preparing to sing Christmas carols on Beacon Hill. Or maybe what motivated me was shame at the fact that of all the languages I had been exposed to up to that point—some eight or nine, I guess—the only one I had failed to learn well was my own ancestral tongue.

I had actually been sent, shortly before I turned thirteen (over my father's scandalized protests), to be prepared for Bar Mitzvah. But I stubbornly resisted learning Hebrew—spending most of my lesson time haranguing the rabbi, who sought to instruct me, about Jewish discrimination against Negroes in America and Arabs in Palestine; or trying to explain to him why all religions, including his own, were the opium of the people. To all of this he would retort only that I read Hebrew "like a cossack"; which was, alas, true.

Indeed, I still read the Holy Tongue like a cossack, even after the valiant efforts of Robert Pfeiffer, the eminent biblical scholar who was my teacher at Harvard, and who did his best to teach us "proper" pronunciation, insisting over and over (for the benefit of the few Jews in the class) that "Hebrew was not a dialect of Polish Yiddish." It was, in any case, pronunciation, grammar, and lexicography in which he believed. Of the mythic import of the text he said little except that it was not, as Christian theologians insisted, a prophecy of Christ's vicarious atonement for the sins of mankind, and that the "Suffering Servant" was Israel—as should be clear to anyone who understood the tenses of the verbs.

But in what the myth of the Suffering Servant might mean after the rise and fall of Hitler, Professor Pfeiffer was not interested. I, however, was, having come begrudgingly and at long last to recognize the full scope and horror of the Holocaust, of which I had for so long remained at least half-deliberately unaware. Before America's entry into World War II, I had dismissed the skimpy, garbled newspaper accounts of the Nazi persecution and slaughter of European Jewry as propaganda:

"atrocity stories," like those about the poor Belgians and the rabid Huns, which had circulated during World War I—and intended, like those, to brainwash the exploited masses into supporting a conflict that would mean more profits for their exploiters and death for them.

Such imperialist wars, I continued to believe even after I had lost faith in Stalin's Soviet Union and had begun to entertain doubts about Marxism-Leninism itself, were the ultimate evil threatening humanity. I was therefore proud that during the thirties I had stood shoulder to shoulder with my fellow students at New York University, crying aloud the "Oxford Oath"; which is to say, vowing that we would never support our own country in any war. Moreover, even as we shouted our resolve, we hoped, believed, that simultaneously massed protesters were echoing our words not only throughout our own country and those of our so-called allies, but even in those lands that a hypocritical F.D.R. (promising peace, but plotting war) had labeled our "enemies." Really, however, we were convinced the "enemy" was the ruling class of one's own country. That is why we sang over and over as we marched the streets of our cities and towns in the years between the Great Wars:

> In seventeen we went to war,
> In seventeen we went to war,
> In seventeen we went to war,
> Didn't know what we were fighting for.
> Time to turn those guns the other way.

So too we stubbornly resisted the argument that Hitler's planned extermination of the Jews made possible a moral distinction between the capitalist Third Reich (where, after all, multinational corporations like Krupp continued to prosper) and the rival capitalist powers, including our own. To grant this, we believed, was also to grant that our imperialist war against Hitler was a just one. It was a notion that most American Jews found easier to believe than did their Jewish brethren in Russia, where anti-Semitism had long since become a weapon in Stalin's struggle for power, or in France, where the Dreyfus case was still a living memory—or even in England, where every schoolchild grew up haunted by the nightmare figures of Shylock and Fagin.

Consequently, those of us self-styled "revolutionaries" who were also Jewish Americans considered it important to keep pointing out that the Jews were merely one target of Hitler's campaign of extermination, which also included gypsies, Poles, homosexuals, the congenitally malformed, Jehovah's Witnesses—and, especially, especially, Communists. To contend otherwise, we felt, would be to play into the hands of the capitalist warmongers like those well-to-do allrightniks whom we had always despised: those former bootleggers and sweatshop owners, who sought to prove that they were good Americans as well as good Jews by simultaneously launching Liberty Bond campaigns and raising money on behalf of Zionism. Which was worse I would then have been hard put to say—their offensively blatant American patriotism or their equally egregious pledges of allegiance to a nation state that did not yet exist.

Even after I had ceased to be a Marxist, their Zionism seemed to me especially offensive, for the last thing an already atomized world needed, I was convinced, was one more nation state. Because of the blessing-curse of exile from their original homeland, the Jews, it seemed to me, had been peculiarly well-suited to play a leading role in the inevitable progress toward a world without borders, flags, and ethnic divisions. The dream of a return to Zion, translated from the mystical to the political sphere, could, however, only eventuate in a society in which there would be not only Jewish statesmen and bureaucrats, but Jewish cops and soldiers—Jewish cossacks, in short. That in turn (as it needed no prophet returned from the grave to foresee) would breed an answering nationalism in the Arab inhabitants of what was to them also the "Holy Land," whom the new settlers would have to dispossess or displace. And to the ensuing Holy War, with mythic roots on both sides, there would be no end.

For a while, as the ensuing drama of terror and counterterror unfolded, I was tempted—following the Communist and Trotskyist line—to side in that struggle with the Arabs, who preferred (like the American Indians, with whom I could not help identifying them) poverty, disorganization, even tyranny under a regime of their coreligionists, to prosperity, law and order, and a modicum of democracy under the auspices of colonizers whose technology, culture, and myths were utterly alien to their own. But I have ended by crying out—without ever ceasing to wish that the remnant of Israel in the Middle East survive and flourish—a curse on both your houses; though, of course, I would prefer to wish on both the blessing of universal brotherhood.

Clearly this has not come to pass in the land of Israel, nor indeed anywhere in the world; and it does not seem likely to come to pass in the foreseeable future. Yet it has not been easy for me to confess that I, who in the first quarter century of my life was sure that (if I lived so long) I would live to see a global *oecumene* without ethnic distinction, have instead lived long enough to see, as I prepare to begin my fourth quarter of a century, a world that atomizes rather than unites: a congeries of self-imposed ghettoes, in which the chief sources of political dynamism are particularism, parochialism, and sectarianism.

Perhaps I surmised all this (though I did not yet have the words to say it to myself) as early as 1942, when I enlisted in the war I had so long anticipated with fear and loathing. Let me be clear. I was not drafted but volunteered, though I was at that point married, with a first child and a second well on the way; and I kept volunteering until I finally ended up at Iwo Jima, in the midst of what not only I came to think of as the mythological culmination of that bloody conflict. But *why?* is the question I still cannot answer.

I was prompted not, I think, by an indifference bred of despair after my discovery that the world had turned out so utterly different from what I had expected. Nor did I act as I did because, as I sometimes told those who asked, I could not endure refusing pusillanimously to share the key experience of my generation. Perhaps it was only that I wanted to escape from what I had begun to feel as the restrictions of premature maturity. Or maybe I just wanted to learn another language; and the program promised not only to make me a commissioned officer in the Navy but to teach me Japanese. This would, however, take me to the remote Pacific—which is to say, at the farthest possible remove from the threatened Jews in Europe. It was there, at any rate, I finally found myself, listening to reports of what was happening on the other side of the world as if they were events on another planet. Though I did listen to those reports in Honolulu, on Guam, and in China, I could not help wishing—I feel obliged to confess—for the defeat of our own expeditionary forces and those of our Russian allies, unable to forget what I had learned too well in my years of Marxist indoctrination: that it was the defeat of the Russians in the First World War that had helped make possible the first successful Socialist Revolution.

I did not, of course—like the defeated soldiers of the Czar —turn my guns the other way: since without ever having fired a gun in any direction, I ended up as one of the victorious. When, therefore, I found myself at the war's end, helmeted and in full battle gear, marching down the streets of a "liberated" Chinese city, I felt like some Hollywood version of a conquering

Nazi entering Paris. So, too, grilling terrified and filthy POWs, I seemed to myself more like an SS interrogator than a Jew-boy from Newark, trapped in a war in which he did not believe; but never more so than when, flanked by a pair of offensively trim commanding officers, I helped capture an alleged "war criminal": a pudgy Japanese businessman who (quite like, I could not help thinking, a Jew trying to pass as a gentile to escape the gas chambers) had disguised himself as a Chinese. He had castrated a coolie, we learned from "a reliable in-formant," and had buried in his backyard a treasure in gold coins. But there was, it turned out, no treasure of any kind, which led me to suspect that the mutilated coolie might have been a fiction as well.

I went therefore to the prison to which my war criminal had been taken to ask whether there might have been some mistake, and I was told that the mistake was mine, that no such person had ever been incarcerated, or indeed existed at all. It is an incident I have never forgotten, though, quite as if, indeed, he had really never existed, I cannot recall his face. What has continued to haunt my dreams ever since, however, is the painted face of the little girl (his adopted "daughter," he assured us, as my Chinese companions smirked) into whose hands he thrust a farewell gift, breaking temporarily from our grasp, as she kept screaming his name—which I have also forgotten. Another scene from a wartime propaganda film, in which I am once more hopelessly miscast.

Small wonder that long before I was finally shipped home I had come to identify with the Japanese rather than my American comrades-in-arms, whom I had seen performing not only acts of valor that put me to shame, but also atrocities: brutally beating disarmed prisoners, for instance, or stopping long enough under fire of their living enemies to extract with their bayonets the gold teeth of those dying or already dead. I never doubted for a moment that had I seen the Japanese as victors I would have witnessed equally atrocious acts. But I encountered them only as victims: and as victims, all men, I came then to believe, are the suffering servants through whose stripes their victimizers are healed—are, in the mythological sense, Jews.

Real Jews, however, were as rare on shipboard and the islands of the Pacific as they had been in Montana; but when I finally got to China—which is to say, when my long westward flight from my ancestral past had reached the ultimate East—I encountered, to my surprise, genuine Jewish refugees from European terror. They had not fled the Nazis, though, these loudmouthed hustlers in tight-waisted sports jackets, with whom I chatted over Sunday morning bagels and tea at the Imperial Hotel in Tientsin. Nor had the more soberly garbed burghers-in-exile, like the soft-spoken old gent who invited me home to show off his dog, who understood Yiddish, and his Hebrew prayerbook autographed by Eleanor Roosevelt.

It was the Bolshevik Revolution from which they had run in 1917 and were running still, side by side with goyim, to whom the new regime was equally threatening. But the goyish and Jewish expatriates in Tientsin had almost nothing to do with each other, the former socializing with their own kind in the White Russian Club (some of their rebellious children had already split off to form a Red one), while the latter gathered in what they called, of course, the *Kunst*, the Art Club.

The only art practiced there, however, was—as far as I could tell on a single visit—money changing. But, after all, a Jew has to live; and what else was there to do for these stateless wanderers, except maybe peddle contraband on streetcorners or run on a shoestring some sleazy brothel-saloon. Nonetheless, I could not despise or condescend to—much less, God forbid, pity—these *luftmenschen* without a past or a future. Undefeated and undismayed, they were capable still of a kind of ironical acceptance of their fate that made me feel childishly naive in my alternating fits of euphoria and despair.

I shall never forget, for instance, the time I made the mistake of saying "thank you" to one of them, after he had given me in exchange for a single U.S. dollar several thousand *yuan*, or whatever the local inflated currency was called. For an instant he regarded me in astonishment, then, shrugging his shoulders and looking up at the heavens, shouted (in an accent that reminded me heartbreakingly of my grandfather's), "Look at him. He gives me good American money. I give him shitpaper, and he says thank you." At that point, I knew that I had still a *goyisher kopf*, perhaps would never be a real Jew.

Nevertheless, quite as if I were one, I joined in conversations with those who were about the persecution of "our people" by Russians and Ukrainians and Poles. As far as I can remember, however, we never talked about the atrocities inflicted by the Nazis on their fellows who had remained behind in the *shtetlach* from which they had fled. Perhaps, once more like my grandfather, they could associate such murderous violence only with their traditional enemies, the Slavs; or maybe what was happening in a Europe in which they could no longer quite believe had remained for them as invisible and unreal as it was for me.

It became realer, however, once I had returned to America, where the full horror of the Holocaust was, I soon discovered, being relentlessly documented in print, on stage and screen, radio and TV. There was, therefore, no way in which I could avoid becoming aware not just of that horror but of the shame it triggered in me for having for so long (deliberately? half-deliberately?) remained unaware of it. My first response, though, to that belated awareness was not pity or terror, but rage: a blind rage directed at first not—consciously at least—at myself, but at all the people of Germany, living or dead. For a long while, I would scream at anyone who attempted, however innocently, to address me in German, "I do not speak the language of Hitler!" forgetting that it was also the language of Kafka, whose *The Castle* I had, at age seventeen, painfully read in the original, not knowing that it had already been translated into English.

That visceral, irrational anger was further exacerbated by the fact that a catastrophe that had been labeled in an instant cliché "unspeakable" was being not only spoken about everywhere, but packaged, hyped, and sold on the marketplace: Anne Frank's memoirs, for instance, became overnight a best-seller, and the Nuremburg Trials were translated almost immediately from the headlines to the movie screen. The motives of the publishers and producers were, quite obviously, crassly commercial, which was bad enough, but what prompted their paying audiences, both Jewish and gentile, was, I could not help feeling, something worse: on the one hand, a kind of sadomasochistic voyeurism, which they did not confess even to themselves; and on the other, a desire, which they have easily confessed, to assuage the guilt they suffered for their earlier blindness.

That covert relish of horror pornography I shared, as well as that guilt, plus the added shame of being, though a Jew, an unscathed survivor. Nonetheless, I stubbornly resisted seeing any of those films or reading any of those books, because, I told myself, the vicarious atonement they afforded was too easy, too cheap. I was afraid, moreover, that seeking in such secondhand fictions—only print on the page or images on the screen, no matter how "true to life"—a substitute for the experience I had never really shared would make that experience for me not more but less "real." For similar reasons, I also refused to confront the killers of my people (of all my family that had remained in Europe, I learned on my return, not a single member had survived) on their own home ground. My grandfather's admonition about the dog returning to his vomit had until the war kept me from Europe. But even when in the early fifties I did make the voyage back, eventually living in Europe for two years, I still did not venture into Germany or Poland. Some ten years later, however, convinced that my reluctance was foolishly perverse, I began lecturing and attending literary conferences in Munster and Wurtzburg, Heidelberg and Berlin, finally even Munich, the very heart of Hitlerdom. Inevitably, I was asked by the German academics I encountered, their guilts obviously deeper than mine, "Why did we do it? Only we Germans could have done it, no?"; to which I was able to answer at that point, almost, almost believing it, "If you could have done it, *anyone* could."

In smugly, offensively prosperous Munich, however, my rage was kindled once more; so that crying out (as my ancestors had for generations) "Why do the wicked prosper?" I fled to nearby Dachau. It was not tearful compassion or nauseated revulsion I experienced, however, visiting my first and last concentration camp—only a sense of anticlimax, so nearly comic that I came close to laughing out loud. The spankingly trim barracks and gas chambers, I soon discovered, were not the originals, where real Jews had really bled and died; but a scrupulously reconstructed ersatz—like the restorations of bombed-out medieval churches at which I had gawked earlier. Finally, in the midst of giggling schoolchildren, shepherded by grimly serious teachers, and bored sightseers just off the bus, I felt myself not a pilgrim to a place of martyrdom but a tourist in some horrific Disneyland.

Consequently, I returned with actual relief to the conference on Postmodernism from which I had been playing hooky; though once back, I endured the indignity, as I had everywhere in Germany, of being regarded not just as a representative American but a token Jew. And why not, after all, since—however problematical my Jewishness may have seemed to me—it is as a Jewish-American spokesman for the Jewish-American Renaissance of the fifties and sixties that I have been invited to speak almost everywhere on the face of the globe over the past two or three decades. During those exhilarating years gentile readers in Italy and France, India, Japan and Korea, particularly the younger ones, had been reading Saul Bellow and Bernard Malamud, Allen Ginsberg and Philip Roth in preference to writers in their own languages, feeling somehow that they spoke more directly to them. And they called on critics like me to explain to them why—assuming, of course, that like those writers I was a Jew. Nor did I refuse to play that part.

But I have had a little more difficulty maintaining that role when those who call upon me to bear witnesses are Jewish themselves. The first time, for instance, that I ever visited Israel was as a participant in a symposium of Jewish writers, American and Israeli, at the end of which David Ben-Gurion himself urged me to make *aliyah*. Not only was my life in exile inauthentic, unreal, the then premier told me, but "unless more Jews like you return," he went on to explain, "*they* will eventually outnumber *us*." It was clear that by *they* he meant the Sephardim, the "black Jews," and by "*us*," the Ashkenazim, the "white" ones. Never in my life have I felt less like a Jew, black or white. Nonetheless, I have gone back to Israel five or six times over the years since, only to leave each time further confused and dismayed.

On my latest visit, for example, without quite realizing that it was the Sabbath, I stood outside my hotel to watch Jerusalem turn golden under the setting sun and to smoke a farewell cigar in peaceful meditation. My peace did not last long, however, since almost instantly a group of ultra-Orthodox zealots gathered together across the road to scream Hebrew imprecations at my blasphemy; to which I screamed back, "Don't worship idols!"

—unsure whether this made me more or less Jewish than they. In any case, they understood my English as little as I did their Hebrew, which made it all a sort of bad joke.

My other close encounter with the ultra-Orthodox, however, was no joke, good or bad, though it too exacerbated my lifelong identity crisis. I had been invited in the early seventies to a private audience with the Lubavitcher Rebbe, who, it was evident from the first, assumed that I was a Jew. Certainly, it was as a Jew that he gave me his message, which was "The house is burning. Save the children!" Nonetheless, when he went on to ask me for my name, I was confused enough to answer "Leslie Fiedler"; and only after he had shaken his head rather ruefully did I confess that my Hebrew name was "Eliezar," my mother's in the same tongue "Leah"—that I was, therefore, as he understood reality, really, *really* Eliezar ben Leah. Under that name, at any rate, he promised to ask a blessing for me when he next talked to his predecessor, who had been dead for twenty years.

I was not churlish enough to say, though I could not help feeling, that I, Leslie Fiedler once more, believed in no blessings from beyond the grave; and that in any case I needed no such blessing, since I had already been blessed by the living: by the gentiles among whom I have made my career. Like him, they had assumed I was a Jew; and, seeking to make amends for the Holocaust, they have opened up to me—along with other Jewish Americans of my generation—academic posts and cultural distinctions, access to which had earlier been barred to those descended from the Killers of Christ. I have, that is to say, profited from a philo-Semitism as undiscriminating as the anti-Semitism in reaction to which it originated. And to make matters worse, I have shamelessly played the role in which I have been cast, becoming a literary Fiedler on the roof of academe.

But in what sense, though, I am really the representative Jew for which I have been taken, I have long asked myself, and ask myself still at age seventy-plus. "It's hard to be a Jew," my grandfather used to tell me; and from childhood on I have taken this to be an essential aspect of Jewish identity. For me, however, after that single scare of my childhood, it has all been only too easy. Ever since, anti-Semitism has been something I read about in the papers, what happens to someone else. Even in this negative sense, therefore, I can lay no claim to being really Jewish; and even less can I lay a positive one, being bereft of all *yiddishkeit* and almost entirely ignorant of rabbinic lore. What I know of the Five Books of Moses I know in King James English. Indeed, English is not just my *mammeloshen* but my *lashon-ha-kaddish* as well. My Holy Books, though no longer *Das Kapital* and *What Is to Be Done?* as in my youth, or *The Waste Land* and *The Golden Bowl* as in my early manhood, are in my declining years not the Torah and Talmud but *Huckleberry Finn* and the *Collected Plays of Shakespeare*.

Moreover, I have never in my life put on tefillin or attached a mezuzah to the doorpost of my house. Nor have I ever joined a Jewish congregation or fraternal order. In this, to be sure, I am like my father and grandfather, who also rejected all outward signs and symbols of Jewish belonging. In fact, the only religiously observant member of my family I ever knew was my paternal great-grandfather, the first of my seed to have been buried in American soil. I had met him, however, only once or twice (neither of us understanding the language of the other) before his funeral, where an equally pious friend of his delivered—in their language, not mine—a graveside sermon that set the mourners to weeping and screaming.

What they were crying and screaming about, however, I did not learn until much later, when an aunt interpreted for me. What grandpa's friend had said, she explained, was that he had suffered the worst indignity a good Jewish father could endure, seeing some of his children die before him; and this was because he had permitted those doubly accursed children to abandon their ancestral faith in the heathen New World. That they had indeed abandoned that faith became ever more evident as the years passed. The funeral service, for instance, of my father's only brother, who had married not one but two shikses, was held in a Methodist church; and his son's sons do not even know that their ancestors were Jews. Small wonder then that the children and grandchildren of my brother, who has long since become a Lutheran, are similarly ignorant of their roots.

Moreover, not a single one of my own eight children has at the present moment a Jewish mate; nor, for that matter, do I. Most of those kids, it is true, still think of themselves as in some vestigial sense Jews. But of my six grandsons only three have been circumcised—and one of those primarily because such ritual wounding is a part of the ancestral traditions of his Ashanti father. In any case, there is no one to say kaddish for me when I die. I am, in short, not just as I have long known, a minimal Jew—my Judaism nearly nonexistent—but, as I have only recently become aware, a terminal one as well, the last of a four-thousand-year line. Yet whatever regrets I may feel, I cannot deny that I have wanted this, worked for it. From childhood on, I dreamed a world without ethnic or religious divisions, though I knew that this meant a world without Jews.

What I did not suspect was that, ironically, in my lifetime half of that dream would begin to come true, reminding me of an aphorism of Goethe I should not have forgotten: "Be careful of what you wish for in your youth, because you will get it in your old age." What I have lived to see is a world in which even as sectarianism and anti-Semitic violence flourish in certain gentile communities, an ever larger segment of Jewry is losing its ethnic identity. Such attrition through intermarriage and assimilation has not, of course, been confined only to my own family—or even just to the United States, in which we are far from atypical. It is evident wherever large numbers of Jews continue to live in exile: particularly, perhaps, in England and the Commonwealth nations, but also throughout Western Europe, South America, and the Soviet Union, where refuseniks are the exception rather than the rule.

But none of this excuses my own complicity in what those who deplore it most (those observant Jews, who, though a majority, feel threatened and defensive) call with deliberate malice the "Silent Holocaust." That pejorative epithet I cannot help resenting, preferring neutral terms like "acculturation" or "assimilation"—even "apostasy." Finally, however, I must grant that the implicit comparison of the "Final Solution" I have abetted to Hitler's is hyperbolic perhaps, but not entirely unjustified. Both propose, that is to say, an end to a separate Jewish identity, whether defined racially, religiously, or culturally.

To be sure, our "Holocaust" is not imposed from without by brute force but freely chosen. Moreover, it is not motivated by hatred (not even self-hatred, as is sometimes charged) but by love: a love of all humanity, including those who have long persecuted us. Finally, we unreconstructed assimilationists, unlike the Nazis, seek not to obliterate along with their bodies the very memory of the Jews, but rather to memorialize in honor the last choice of the Chosen People: their decision to cease to exist in their chosenness for the sake of a united mankind. Still in all, it cannot be denied that the future we have dreamed is, like that foreseen for the "Thousand-Year Reign," *Judenrein*. It is for this reason that I have found it impossible to reflect self-righteously on the Holocaust which left me unscathed, without alluding uneasily to that other which has left me feeling like a Last Jew.

Nonetheless, Last Jew that I am, I cannot resist confessing, in conclusion, that each autumn, though I do not, of course, go to shul, I dutifully observe the fast of Yom Kippur. So, too, each winter, I light the lights of Chanukah, more often than not beside an already lighted Christmas tree. And each spring, after dyeing Easter eggs, I gather my family together for a Passover seder—crying out to the God in whom I do not think I believe, "Pour out your wrath upon the goyim. . . ." My children somehow do not ever ask me why, perhaps because they are sure they already know. If they did ask, however, I would say to them, as my grandfather said to me, sneaking me off to some storefront synagogue on the High Holy Days, "Not because I believe, but so you should remember."

I remember.

Acknowledgments

Earlier versions of the essays in this book were first published or delivered as follows:

"The Roots of Anti-Semitism: A View from Italy": as "Le radici dell'antisemitismo qualche riflessióne dall'Italia," *Ebraismo e antiebraismo: immàgine e pregiudizio*, Giuntina, Firenze, Italy, 1989

"Bloom on Joyce; or, Jokey for Jacob," *Journal of Modern Literature*, Vol. 1, No. 1, 1970

"Joyce and Jewish Consciousness," "Culture, Technology, and Destiny," a seminar in the Celtic Studies department, St. Michael's College, University of Toronto, 1985

"The Christian-ness of the Jewish-American Writer," given at Bar-Ilon University, 1983

"Isaac Bashevis Singer; or, the American-ness of the American-Jewish Writer," *Studies in American Jewish Literature*, ed. Daniel Walden, Albany, State University of New York Press, 1981

"Why Is the Grail Knight Jewish?" *Aspects of Jewish Culture in the Middle Ages*, ed. Paul E. Szarmach, Albany, State University of New York Press, 1979

"Styron's Choice," *Psychology Today*, July 1979. Reprinted with permission from Psychology Today Magazine. Copyright © 1979 PT Partners, L.P.

"Going for the Long Ball," *Psychology Today*, June 1983. Reprinted with per-

mission from Psychology Today Magazine. Copyright © 1983 PT Partners, L.P.
"Growing Up Post-Jewish," *The New York Times Book Review*, May 18, 1986.
Copyright © 1986 by The New York Times Company. Reprinted by permission.
"The Many Names of S. Levin: An Essay in Genre Criticism," *The Fiction of Bernard Malamud*, ed. Richard Astro and Jackson J. Benson, Oregon State University Press, 1977
"A Meditation on the Book of Job," *Congregation: Contemporary Writers Read the Jewish Bible*, ed. David Rosenberg, New York, Harcourt Brace Jovanovich, 1987
"In Every Generation: A Meditation on the Two Holocausts," *Testimony*, ed. David Rosenberg, New York, Times Books, 1989